STILETTOS, SHOPPING & THE F WORD

Why Women Should Care About The Coming Financial Crisis

DIANNA MOSES

Copyright © 2018 Dianna Moses

All rights reserved.

ISBN-13: 978-1539589051
ISBN-10: 1539589056

DEDICATION

This book is dedicated to all the spectacular women I have met in my life that work hard, don't take no for an answer and can do anything they set their minds to and do it well! There's a few females that come to mind (in alphabetical order) that have inspired me for this book; I may have borrowed from their fabulous personalities to flush out some characters or used one of their situations as an example but the reality is that my life is better for knowing them. Thanks to Alissa, Astrid, Cynthia, Elisa, Jacque, Jin Sun, Leah, Lisa, Lynda, Karin, Kelley, Kitty, Pinky, Victoria, and the ones I can't name – you know who you are! Additionally I have to thank the women who have inspired me throughout my life and shaped my young mind, for sure Granma! She was the one female constant in my life that always knew just what to say. She didn't have just one amazing marriage but two (the second one at age 83!). But there's other women who I admire for their brazen, bold actions, words and personalities: Mae West, Dorothy Draper, Coco Chanel and Zelda Fitzgerald to name a few.

Here's some words I live by: Be unstoppable. Don't let your gender or age stop you. If you want it; go after it. Make it yours. Do it well. A man is not a financial plan, stop waiting for them to take care of you. Have your own financial goals, your own money and don't settle for anything but the best for yourself. If you don't take care of you, who will? Be kind, but be fierce.

Use this book to get you started on a clear financial path that will give you the freedom to live a happier life. Retirement planning and investing is a complicated world but this should arm you with some information, ideas and questions to ask your financial professional or research on your own. If you don't know where to start, I'm on LinkedIn, drop me a line. I'll always help in any way I can.

CONTENTS

OBJECTIVE i
ARRIVAL 1
IN FOR A SURPRISE 15
A GIFT 35
THE F WORD 52
FASHION 88
THE FUTURE 129
TRUST ME 163
WHAT'S NEXT? 179

OBJECTIVE

My hope is this book, written in story format, will help women discover how they can make changes in their lives to better their financial future. We know without a shadow of a doubt the market will go down; that's what it does: it goes up and it goes down. There will be big corrections like 2008 and if you plan well you can avoid fiscal disaster with careful planning and diversification. Everything in this book is for general ideas of what you can do. My suggestion is, regardless of your background, talk to a financial professional. We've all been on WebMD trying to diagnose ourselves but when it's something important you know you need a medical professional to guide you and the financial world is no exception. There are many options on how to save money and plan for the future and this book will show you some of those and, hopefully change how you think about money. Men brag about their investments. But women? Usually we brag about the buy one get one deal we just snagged but we rarely talk about how we are planning for our retirement income. Start now, no matter your age or situation, start making changes so you can sleep better at night knowing you have a plan in place. Enjoy the book and sit down with a real financial advisor with experience working with people like you to help make those decisions. Good luck and happy reading!

ARRIVAL

I was sitting in a crappy rental car at JFK waiting for a flight from CDG. Actually, let me rephrase that, I was driving around in circles at JFK airport in a crappy rental car because there weren't any open spots in the cell phone lot and Topaz's flight from Paris was delayed. I laughed out loud in the car when I read the board saying DELAYED. That is the way Topaz would have phrased it; planes are never late now, they're *delayed*. It's the same message, but one has a more positive spin. She's always thinking positive.

As a New Yorker I don't own a car; I don't need a car. For me to rent a car and drive out to Queens is a bit extravagant but for me to rent a car to drive to Queens to pick someone up at the airport is completely unheard of! However, it is not every day you get to pick someone up from the airport like my friend Topaz Indigo Morgan aka Tim, plus she's flying in from Charles de Gaulle.... PARIS! I couldn't wait to see her because it's been months since she's been in NY. I had no idea she would be gone this long; although in her defense, neither did she.

Before I go any further I probably should back up a whole lot more. I'm a pretty good storyteller; I'm an attorney, we paint a picture with words for a living. Whether you're building a case or telling a tale, it's always good to provide some background and get everyone up to speed.

I am Melissa Scarpetti, senior staff counsel at a prominent NYC advertising firm. I'm Sicilian, fiery, a little OCD, a recovering workaholic and live in the same building as my friend Topaz. Before you say what kind of flowerchild/stripper name is Topaz, let me just stop you right there – because I went through all of the same reactions when I first met her.

Mind you, I'm calling her my friend even though I really don't know much about her. I mean, I know the important stuff; she changed my life. But I don't really understand what she does for a living, her age, who her friends are (besides me) or any of the basics. What I do know about her is that if I hadn't met her I'd still be a miserable drone at my job or maybe at a different firm and most likely need some heavy doses of Botox to remove my scowl lines.

I haven't heard much from Topaz since she left NYC. Her last note said to me that "something came up" and she was going to Paris for a "few weeks". Well weeks turned into months and here we are: her presumably on a plane in transit and me trying to find parking. I don't know what came over me but I offered to pick her up from the airport. Something about Topaz made you want to just do things for her.

"Holy shit!" I say to the empty rental car. Just as I pulled into the cell phone lot someone was leaving! Apparently just thinking about Topaz gives me good karma. Oh, wait, karma – CARma. Hahaha. I laugh to myself at my pun.

No sooner had I pulled into the spot the big board changes status and shows that her flight has arrived. Of course, that's just how it goes.

I decided to wait for a few minutes for off boarding so that I wouldn't have to continue circling JFK airport waiting for her to arrive. After about 10 minutes I received a text from Topaz telling me where she was and I left the cell phone lot to go retrieve her.

Driving up to the passenger pickup area I spot Topaz talking to a tall, good looking man in a suit and standing next to her was an airline porter guarding her bags as if it was his only mission in life. All three of them were talking excitedly and laughing. Some things never change, I thought. She can make friends with anyone anywhere.

I pull over and pop the trunk of the rental car as I get out. Before I have even reached the other side of the car the porter is already loading Topaz's suitcases into the trunk. When Topaz sees me she squeals with delight and runs over to me with her arms spread wide. She looks different but somehow just the same.

Topaz is wearing a brightly colored red and gold Hermès scarf around her neck and is donning an impeccably crisp tan silk blouse. I'm not sure how she can look so fresh considering she just flew from Paris to NYC and it's now almost 11pm. She is sporting olive drab shorts that also have somehow retained their freshness, ending in a cuff which showcase her tan legs. She is laden with giant jewelry on her wrists and fingers and a giant necklace of crystals are shimmering against her tan blouse. Her long dark hair is up and she's wearing her signature, impossibly high, 5 inch stilettos. Her strappy sandals are gold and olive drab with ankle straps that wrap around her calves like some sort of sexy snake.

I'm not sure I've ever seen an Hermès scarf that looked so vibrant or it could have just been the way it stood out against the earth tones of her outfit. She pulled the whole ensemble off really well and her energy was very apparent.

Normally I would just be in sweats but since I was going to meet Topaz I chose to put on a cute pair of yoga pants and loose knit sweater. For some reason I had assumed she'd be dressed comfortably so she could sleep on the plane but she looked fresh and ready for whatever was next.

I nearly fall over feeling like I had been tackled by an NFL guard when Topaz reaches me with her giant bear hug. A second after that I'm clobbered by a monstrous bag that she had slung on her arm.

"Oh, sorry!" Topaz says while looking anything but sorry.

She held up the bag for me to examine. She apparently acquired an amazing bright red and gold Chanel satchel while in Paris which seemed to be a perfect match for her lipstick and scarf.

"Wow!" I said impressed.

Topaz then looks at me and does a twirling motion with her finger for me to turn around, apparently so she can examine my outfit. I am now regretting not wearing something a little more fashionable.

"You look fantastic! Those yoga pants really suit you!"

"Thank you" I said not really believing her. "You look absolutely amazing. How did you stay so fresh on your flight?"

"I flew first class, of course" she says winking at me.

By now the porter has put all of her bags into the trunk and the man in the suit is just standing there smiling at us and watching our exchange. Topaz thanks the porter and hands him some money with a squeeze of her hand. He takes the money but continues to linger.

The man in the suit seems to be waiting for something and Topaz walked over to him. She fishes a business card out of her bright red bag and hands it to him. I can't hear their exchange but he shakes her hand and smiles.

I notice a Transit Authority cop walking towards us and I know that is my cue to get the vehicle moving. I start heading towards the driver's side of the car and Topaz waves to the porter and the man in the suit. She gets into the passenger side. Once the doors are closed and we are underway Topaz start talking.

"Mon dieu, je suis très fatigué!"

I look over her at her with a puzzled look on my face.

"Oh, I forgot you don't speak French. I just said how tired I am although the flight was really refreshing."

"Refreshing? I thought it was delayed?"

"It was but the delay gave me time to chat with the stewardess; she was really nice. She and I are going to have dinner in two weeks when she is in town next."

It is no surprise to me that Topaz made friends on a flight during the delay portion. While most people would be stressed out she is making the best of an opportunity presented to her to meet a new friend.

"Who is the guy in the suit?"

"That was Derek; he was sitting in the next seat over. He flies back and forth between New York and Paris all of the time on business. He wanted my card. But enough about him how have you been? It is so good to see you! I am so happy to be back in New York!"

"I have been good. Work is going really well and as you know I got the promotion right before you left. It has been a really great opportunity for me because I am not bored at work and I feel like I'm making a difference in some of my colleague's lives."

"That's fantastic news; I'm so happy for you!"

"Thank you. I really am pleased with how things are as well. Are you staying in New York for a while?"

"I have no plans to leave but you know I will go wherever I am needed."

We drove in silence for a few seconds as I think of something else to say. Topaz has been gone for so long there are too many topics to choose from and I'm not very good at small talk. I turn to look at her to ask her about the food in Paris and I realize that she has drifted off to sleep.

I smile to myself remembering the six-hour time difference between New York and Paris and I am glad to learn she is human and is actually tired. I put the radio on a station with some soft music and continue the drive back to our building. I had asked the doorman Bill to secure a parking spot for the night so that it would be easy to move all of her bags into her apartment. It was a bit of a hassle but I am glad I was able to pick her up at the airport. It was great to have Topaz back in town.

At that time of night there was almost no traffic getting back into the City, the whole trip was less than half an hour. Pulling onto our street I woke up Topaz.

"Tim, wake up! We're almost there."

Topaz opened her eyes; suddenly alert.

"I am so sorry to fall asleep on you. What a terrible passenger I am!" Topaz looks at her watch, "Oh, this is the time I would normally be getting up but I haven't slept since yesterday."

She stifles a yawn.

"Don't worry about it."

"I hope you don't mind but can we catch up tomorrow? I spoke to Irina a couple of days ago and she has planned a brunch for us tomorrow. She said she has some exciting news and would not tell me what it is. Besides I want to talk to the two of you; there's so much to discuss! We have oodles of catching up to do."

"No problem. What time tomorrow?"

"Irina wanted us to meet in the lobby at 10am tomorrow, does that sound good?"

I had cleared my entire weekend because I wanted to catch up with Topaz so I was completely open to brunch the next day.

"Yes."

As I pulled in front of our building Bill came walking out with a luggage cart dragging behind him. He practically skipped down the steps and opened the door for Topaz.

"It is so good to see you again Ms Morgan. Ms Scarpetti, it is ok for you to park across the street. I put a cone in front of that parking spot and it is good until 3pm tomorrow."

"Thank you, Bill. I will leave my key with you in case it needs to be moved in the middle of the night."

I use the remote to open the trunk so that he would be able to get at Topaz's luggage. Once all the luggage was on the sidewalk I got back into the car and pulled it across the street to the parking spot that had been reserved for me. By the time I walked back across the street all of her luggage has been put on to the luggage cart and Topaz and Bill were speaking to each other animatedly. When I returned to the building Topaz wished Bill a good night and we started walking.

Topaz and I pushed the giant cart through the lobby and to the elevators. It was obvious that Topaz was really tired and her fresh look was fading very quickly. I followed Topaz to her top-floor apartment and helped her unload the luggage. I told her I would return the cart to the elevator and with that she thanked me and closed the door.

I walked to the elevator with the giant empty luggage cart and wondered what surprise Irina had in store for us. Since Topaz has been gone I haven't really seen Irina much for some reason even though we lived in the same building.

I got back into the elevator and hit the 12 button and the L button. when the elevator dinged to signal I was on the 12th floor I stepped out leaving the luggage cart to return to the lobby to the doorman. I walked back into my apartment also tired and ready for sleep.

• ○ • ○ • ○ •

The next morning I woke up to birds chirping. I have grown accustomed to waking up full of gratitude. Waking up this way has completely changed my life. Before I met Topaz I was always hitting the snooze button and starting my day off exasperated and fatigued. Now I typically wake up before my alarm goes off and have a refreshing start to my morning. I walk into work with a calm attitude and a clear mind.

I listen to the melody of the birds chirping somewhere outside my window and remember excitedly that Topaz is back in town. I glanced at my clock and it is 9:15 am. I better get going I thought to myself. I get up to shower and start getting ready to see Topaz and Irina. About 10 minutes to 10am I walked towards the elevator on my floor and press the down button.

When the elevator arrives it's empty and I step into the car. I am absently humming a tune to myself and am excited about whatever surprise Irina has for us. Once the elevator arrives in the lobby the doors open and I begin to walk down the long marble hallway. I have no idea what Irina has planned for us today but knowing that Topaz has just returned from Paris expect that she will be wearing some amazing outfit; probably more amazing than how she normally looks.

The last time that I went out with Irina and Topaz I looked more like the schoolmarm than a single woman out on the town. Today I am rocking a pair of jeans that fit me absolutely perfect, ballet flats and a blue Ralph Lauren chambray blouse. It is still conservative but I'm at least stylish today. I stroll to the end of the lobby and reach the doorman station.

"Hello, Roland, have you seen Topaz and/or Irina?"

My doorman always looks the same no matter what time of day or night he is working. He is always very polite and remembers everyone's names. I had been living in the building for more than three years before I ever learned his name but now I know almost everyone that works in the building.

"No, Ms Scarpetti, I have not seen either of them yet. There is a car outside waiting for you though."

I look at him questioningly and I'm about to say something when I hear a squeal of delight.

"Darling, you look like you belong in the Hamptons!" says Irina from down the long marble hall.

Irina is a tall, previously blonde Russian who recently changed her hair to a very bright pink. It looks amazing on her, I have to admit. When I first met her I was horrified but now that I see how happy it makes her and have gotten to know her better I realized that this was one of the best moves that she has made for herself in a long time. Irina is wearing brown suede boots that remind me of something Pocahontas might wear and matching brown shorts. She has on a white blouse with sleeves that look like wings. Around her neck is a bright pink necklace that seems to match the color of her hair. She looks amazing as always. I am pretty sure that she is a model or was a model in a past life. Surprisingly I have known Irina for almost a year and I still do not know her last name. About the only thing I do know about her is that she's friends with Topaz and lives on the 18th floor.

"Thank you. You look stunning. Those are very cute boots."

Irina twirls around so I can see her entire outfit and she just looks incredible. She is also very happy and I'm not sure what is different because she's always seemed happy. But today she appeared to have a special energy about her.

In mid-turn Irina spots Topaz coming out of the elevator. Topaz and Irina simultaneously shriek with delight and start rushing towards one another. I watch the two of them slightly amused.

No surprise Topaz is wearing a very chic outfit that looks like it was recently on a Paris fashion runway. She is sporting 5 inch metallic gold platform strappy sandals, a cute pair of camel colored Capri pants and is wearing a dill green silk blouse that seems to be picking up the flecks in her eyes. I have never seen her look quite so vibrant. She has switched handbags to a much smaller bright green number that could be any number of famous designers but I certainly did not recognize it.

Topaz and Irina do double air kisses and hugs. They are both clearly very excited to see each other. They spot me and walk back over to where I stood. I give Irina and Topaz double air kisses as well. Irina can barely contain herself.

"Ladies, I have a huge surprise for us today. I have even rented a car and driver to whisk us away in style."

At this point I remembered the rental car that I had left outside. Glancing at my watch I knew I may not have enough time to get back by 3pm.

"I will catch up with you guys just tell me where we are going. I need to get the rental car back to the place so I'm not charged an extra day."

Irina glances at the doorman. Roland catches Irina's look and you can see him nod.

"I have already taken care of your rental car. Today we worry about nothing."

"What do you mean you've already taken care of the rental car?"

"I had it returned to the rental place down the street, Ms Scarpetti" says Roland. "Irina called down this morning and asked if I would take care of it. I hope you don't mind. I was going to call you but she said not to wake you up."

"Thank you," I said not really sure what else to say. I know that when Irina or Topaz have an idea that it is impossible to argue with the two of them. I have never had a bad time with them and to be honest with myself I was not looking forward to the hassle of returning the rental car and then taking mass transit back.

Irina and Topaz link arms with me and the three of us head down the stairs of our building. As we walk down the stairs the driver in our town car gets out to open the passenger door for us. We all scooched inside and continued giving each other compliments.

"Where we going?" I asked

"Don't worry your pretty little head about it." says Irina. "It's a surprise."

"Of course it is" I say resigned to just go with the flow.

"So don't keep us in suspense, Irina, tell us what your surprise is! I know it's more than just a destination."

Irina pats Topaz's knee and says "Don't worry your pretty head about it, Tim" and starts laughing.

Topaz just grins and the driver zooms up the West Side Highway on our way to Destination Unknown.

IN FOR A SURPRISE

Topaz, Irina and I all make small talk on the drive to Irina's secret location. I wonder what could be so important that Irina wants to rent a limo and take us to a brunch, especially when we could have just taken an Uber. Topaz is excitedly telling us about a boutique she found in Paris. She insists that we all come back to her apartment sometime this weekend so she can show us all the special pieces she was able to "acquire".

The driver pulls into a restaurant that I had never been to before but I had been hearing good things about. It sits on the Hudson River and the morning sun was sparkling brightly at us. He pulls up front and gets out to open the driver's side passenger door while the restaurant doorman opens the passenger's side door.

The three of us get out and walk down the carpet towards the entrance of the restaurant. Another doorman opens the front door to the restaurant for us and we walk into a dazzling lobby. The chandelier is modern with Swarovski crystals everywhere and there is bright light coming in from the river view side. Irina walks up to the hostess and gives her name to the woman. Apparently she was expecting us because we are immediately seated.

Moments after we sat at our table a server appears and nods at Irina. He asked if we would like sparkling or still water. Almost in unison we all reply sparkling and giggle that we're all on the same page. It is nice to be back together.

Moments later another server appears with a bucket brimming with ice and sits it on a stand next to our table. Topaz and I look at each other wondering what it's for and Irina is looking at us like the cat that ate the canary. She has a grin on her face that is in danger of splitting her face in half.

The original server reappears with a tray containing a bottle of sparkling mineral water as well as three glasses for us and a plate of limes. He expertly pours our glasses and puts the half empty bottle on the table; completely ignoring the ice bucket. I pick up my water glass and hold it in the air.

"Cheers!"

Topaz and Irina look at each other and back to me with disapproval.

"We don't toast with water." Topaz says.

"Ever" Irina says in agreement.

I give them both a look, shrug and drink my sparkling water anyway.

As we are sipping our mineral waters, the server reappears with a bottle in hand and a linen napkin covering his arm.

"Good morning, ladies. My name is Eric and I will be taking care of you today. May I present to you this lovely bottle of Veuve Clicquot La Grande Dame Brut Rosé."

With a flourish of his white linen napkin he displays the beautiful black and pink bottle. Topaz and Irina both giggle with anticipation. I remember this bottle from one night at Topaz's apartment when we all had only just first met.

"Is this included with brunch?" I ask.

"No," Eric replies, "Ms Petrovia called yesterday to special order it for this occasion." He pronounced Petrovia with a Russian accent as if he had hailed from Mother Russian.

Now I know her last name, I thought. I repeated her name in my head Irina Petrovia, she sounded famous.

Irina looks at Eric and says something in Russian. It was clearly a question and you could tell Eric was pleased with his answer. She said something else to him in her native tongue and smiled. She then turned back to us.

"I thought this was fitting. If you're going to drink champagne it should be good and if you're going to drink a rosé it may as be Veuve Clicquot. Of course, if a la Grande Dame is available you should insist upon it."

Topaz and I are watching Eric expertly untwist the cage. Once removed he kept the cork covered with the white napkin at all times. With a small pop, the cork is off and he placed it on a small plate near Irina.

Irina twirls it around in her hands and opens her handbag. With a grin she drops the cork into the bag and zips it closed. I thought this action was unusual because Irina didn't strike me as someone particularly sentimental and she has had this vintage on a number of occasions.

Eric is filling our crystal flutes with the pink liquid careful that the bubbles never overflow.

"The nectar of goddesses!" exclaims Topaz as she watches the tiny bubbles race to the top of our flutes.

Eric finished filling out flutes and placed the champagne into the ice bucket.

"I will be back shortly with your menus."

We all stared at the bubbly pink liquid in the crystal flutes in front of us. I was waiting for Irina to tell us her news. If there was news, I thought, this brunch may have been the surprise; that and the amazing champagne she had pre-ordered. Topaz broke the silence.

"I am so thankful to be here. Irina, this restaurant is beautiful and I can't think of a better way for us to catch up then with you two and some rosé champagne. To Irina!"

She raises her glass and I follow suit.

"Not yet! I have news!"

Irina says excitedly. Topaz and I both lower are glasses.

"As you know, David and I have been seeing a lot of each other lately."

Actually I didn't know she had been seeing anyone seriously. Although I had seen her in the lobby with an Israeli looking gentleman quite a few times and considering she pronounced his name Da-veed, I was pretty sure that was him.

"Yes! You have to tell us everything!" says Topaz, listening intently.

"Well —"

"Irina, you're blushing!"

I looked and she did seem to be flushed. Irina giggles and nods her head, her smile growing larger.

"Yes, he's fantastic. He's ex-Mossad, you know and now owns an executive protection company. I feel so safe around him; like I never have before. It's wonderful."

Topaz and I both say aww and tell her we're happy for her. Irina continues.

"On Wednesday night, David and I were walking along the Promenade. It was such a perfect night. The moon was incredibly bright and as we were walking hand in hand, I stopped him and told him how happy I was being with him. When I said that his face went kind of blank and he said very seriously, 'I've been meaning to talk to you about that.' When he said that I felt my heart drop to my stomach."

"Oh, no! I'm so sorry, Irina. Maybe he will change his mind." I said. I can't believe he broke up with her on a moonlit walk, I thought.

"No, Melissa. Everything is fine. In fact he turned to me and looked deeply into my eyes and says 'I was thinking there is no one else I'd rather spend the rest of my life with.' He then got on one knee and asked me to marry him!"

"What!? Congratulations!!!" Topaz screams. She gets up and gives Irina a hug. I get up too and give her a big squeeze. While we are standing, Topaz grabs her flute and raises it in the air.

"To living happy!"

"To living happy!" Irina and I both say and we clink are flutes together and all sip the fantastic champagne. As the bubbles slide down my throat, the other patrons, sensing our excitement, are all raising their glasses also and the staff is clapping. Irina turns to the rest of the restaurant, does a tiny bow and says thank you, raising her glass to everyone and we all take another sip.

The three of us sit back down and Eric comes to our table and tells Irina congratulations as he places our menus in front of us.

"Is there a ring?"

Irina is still holding her flute and she wiggles her fingers in front of us showing off a beautiful diamond engagement ring. The ring is amazing especially against the pink colored champagne.

"That's gorgeous!" I say, "Your diamond almost looks pink against the champagne. "

"Oh my God, Irina, is that a pink diamond?"

Irina seems to blush again and she puts her flute down on the table. She spreads her hand against the white tablecloth and now it is obvious that there is definitely a pink hue to the beautiful stone. I'm not sure if it was the sunlight or the crystal flutes but I don't think I've ever seen a diamond that sparkled more.

"Yes, it does have a pink tone to it. I couldn't be happier if I had picked it out myself."

"David obviously knows your tastes very well."

I nod in agreement. Now it is Topaz's turn to start speaking.

"I had so much news to tell you but now it all seems to pale in comparison. I am so happy for you, Irina."

Clearly enjoying all the accolades, Irina smiles and takes another sip of champagne.

Eric returns to the table and refills our champagne and water glasses. Looking at our unopened menus he says.

"The chef would like to indulge you in a celebratory brunch today if you'd allow us the pleasure."

We all look at each other and one by one hand back our menus in silent agreement.

"Thank you." says Irina beaming at the waiter.

"It is our pleasure." and he returns to the kitchen. Topaz continues speaking.

"Irina this is such wonderful news. I am so happy that you waited to tell the two of us together so that we can celebrate your joy. It goes hand-in-hand with what I wanted to talk to you about today anyway. Surprising how things work out like that."

Topaz's eyes twinkle as she looks at us.

"Tell us about Paris!" I said.

"Paris is wonderful, as you know, it is one of my favorite cities on Earth. I missed you guys though. I was thinking about you a lot. "

"Awww. We missed you too." I said.

Irina nodded in agreement and raised her champagne in a silent toast.

"While I was over there it gave me a lot of time to reflect on my career practices and how I want to help people in the future. Currently, I work primarily with men which is disappointing because I could be helping so many women. Don't get me wrong, the men I work with are very successful, physicians, athletes, entrepreneurs and others that have high earning potential but —"

I interrupted.

"Tim, I don't mean to cut you off, but I actually don't know what you do, I know it vaguely has something to do with money. I've always been curious but have never had a chance to ask."

Topaz looks at me grinning.

"I'm in financial services. I'm a wealth manager and financial planner."

"Finance?" I make a face. "The F word!"

"I know. Topaz, you're such a lovely person, I can't believe you do the most boring job in the world." Irina chimes in.

"What?" Topaz looks at us with shock. "How can the two of you say that? Having your finances in order is what will allow you to have the freedom to do whatever you want!"

"Luckily for me I don't have to worry about it. I make decent money and David's business is very successful. He comes from a very wealthy family and is an only child. I never want to think about money and now I don't have to plan."

Topaz stares at Irina blankly for a moment.

"I don't even know what to say, Irina, you're a successful computer programmer and I know you make good money. Why would you leave your future finances up to David?"

"I have money. Up until now I wasn't sure that it was enough for me to retire on but now that I'm getting married I don't have to worry about that anymore."

I am nodding in agreement. I have thought the same thing.

Topaz look at the two of us with astonishment. She seems stunned.

"What are you talking about? Both of you are strong, independent women. You are both successful and you're not thinking about your finances? Irina, you of all people, know that a man is not a financial plan."

"Tim, why should I worry? I'm still young and I have my own money. It's not like I'm going to quit working and just let him support me."

"Irina, have I ever steered you wrong or given you bad advice?"

"No, usually bad ideas are mine." With this statement Irina winks and takes another sip of her champagne.

"I'm serious. Do you believe that I have your best interest at heart?"

"Mais, Oui! There's no doubt in my mind you want only the best for me."

"Then promise me in the next couple of weeks you and I sit down and really map out your finances. We can list all of your investments and assets and I can recommend an estate attorney for you. We can set up a trust for you and really create a safe, secure retirement plan for you."

"A trust? Why do I need a trust? Why would I do any of this before getting married? It's not like we're going to do a prenup."

I speak up at this point, although I don't do family law, I do know the value of a prenup.

"Irina, maybe you should think about doing a prenup."

"I think that's a terrible idea and it actually upsets me to even think about doing so. Creating a prenup just as we're about to start our lives together signals that I don't trust that it will last forever. I wouldn't be getting married if I didn't think that we will be together forever. I would like to just stop talking about this altogether!"

Topaz put her hand gently on Irina's. She looks at her with compassion.

"I understand, Irina. I am not trying to rain on your parade. I believe you are making a wonderful choice with David and I am very happy for you. Even if you don't want a prenup or trust prior to marriage, you really need to have a talk with David about money. Talking about your financial situations, spending habits, investment styles and goals for the future with your partner before getting married will be very helpful. You said he's very successful but do you know how much debt he has or his company? Do you know what his credit report is or if he has outstanding issues with the IRS?"

Irina is silently shaking her head no.

Topaz continues "You will feel empowered and more secure if you address these money matters now. You are protecting yourself. As a business person, David will respect that and I'd be surprised if he hasn't already done the same thing. You never know what the future holds. There could be a lawsuit or debt or even taxes that jeopardize your financial future. The money that you have prior to the marriage is not considered community property in most states so protecting it makes sense. I don't know where you plan on living in the future but once you begin to co-mingle your assets and have joint accounts it most likely would be considered marital property."

"That sounds like a lot of work and very emotionally draining. More importantly, talking about money isn't romantic at all."

"Neither is entering a contract of marriage blindly. Do you know if David or his family has a trust set up already? Have you discussed how his business is structured?"

"No, I've never asked." Irina looked embarrassed.

"Irina, that's ok. You just got engaged. There is plenty of time to ask these questions. Have you talked about how your incomes will be split and how bills are going to be paid? Will you be part of his business? Will he make you a partner?"

"Why do you keep bringing up all of these questions? It's like you are planning that we will fail." Irina sounded frustrated and defensive.

Luckily Eric arrived with two other servers in tow holding big trays. He removed the gold chargers from our table and replaced them with a beautiful plate showcasing the most scrumptious looking Eggs Benedict I'd ever seen. He also set out chopped boiled egg whites, chopped yolks, onions, crème fraiche, caviar, three mother of pearl spoons, toast points, capers, smoked salmon, peeled pears, honey, butter and buckwheat blinis. He asked if it was satisfactory and we all enthusiastically assured him it was and he returned to the kitchen.

It all looked so amazing, I didn't know what to try first. With a flurry of activity we were all loading up our plates excited to try everything. Our Eggs Benedicts were quickly consumed and we were now making tiny plates of caviar and smoked salmon. Topaz speaks up.

"Irina, remember that yellow nail polish you bought after getting a manicure? The one that matched those yellow pumps and your handbag?"

Topaz had caught Irina mid-bite. She was nodding.

"Yes, the Deborah Lippmann Walking on Sunshine. Wasn't it perfect? I had that charity brunch that weekend and I was afraid I was going to chip a nail so I bought it in case I needed a touchup. I didn't need it, of course, but I never would have been able to match that shade."

Topaz was nodding. "It did match your ensemble perfectly." Topaz took a sip of champagne. Topaz continued.

"Remember that crazy pink key you gave me?"

"My spare? Of course, just in case I ever lost my purse I wanted to still be able to get into my apartment without calling maintenance so I had a spare made."

"Remember last summer how after we saw that car fire you made me come with you to the hardware store to buy a fire extinguisher?"

"Haha. I know! What was I thinking? There are fire extinguishers all over the building and it isn't like I cook….."

Irina trailed off; suddenly lost in thought.

Topaz just sat there silently, watching Irina. She finished her champagne and Eric appeared from nowhere and refilled her glass and topped off ours finishing the bottle. Irina speaks up again.

"Oh. I see what you're getting out with those examples. The spare nail polish, me giving you my spare key, the fire extinguisher – they're all for 'just in case' situations. Even though I probably will never use them."

"Yes, exactly. We plan for everything. Band-Aids in your medicine cabinet, baking soda by the stove in case of a grease fire, disability insurance, packing an extra outfit on a trip – all of these are examples of things we do all the time planning for the unexpected. Not having candles or a flashlight is almost reckless if you live in an area with frequent electrical outages. As a responsible adult there are just things you do to make sure that if a crisis strikes, you're prepared. For some reason, though, when it comes to marriage, women, especially, don't want to think about the what-if scenarios."

I had never thought about it like that. Topaz really made a good point.

"Well, that's because this is love. He really is my Prince Charming."

"Disney fucked us." Topaz mutters rolling her eyes.

I nearly spit out my food. "What?!"

"Growing up didn't you hear about how Prince Charming was going to come in and sweep us off our feet and we'd live happily ever after? I mean Cinderella's Prince Charming even showed up with shoes!"

"True." I conceded. I really did believe that as a woman I'd never really need to worry about money. That everything would just take care of itself.

"I'm not sure Disney is entirely to blame."

"Well, of course not, but this is not our Grandparent's generation. We go to college, we have careers, we live on our own and we create our own success. What isn't being addressed is what happens later? Are we preparing to take care of our future selves?"

"I never thought about it like that." Said Irina. I nodded in agreement.

"People hate to think about bad things happening so they almost always underestimate the likelihood of them occurring. I once had a client who came to me when her husband filed for divorce. They had been married for 8 years, when he started cheating on her. The two of them had an extremely lavish lifestyle. He came from an exceptionally prominent family and was a trust fund baby. She, on the other hand, was a self-made multi-millionaire. When they met she was making well over $1M dollars a year. His trust only paid him out around $200,000 annually. She did not want to change her lifestyle that dramatically so they began spending mostly her money."

"When they went to go buy a vacation home they took half a million dollars out of her investments and used it for the purchase. Even though it was all her money, they put both of their names on the title of the house. In fact over the course of the marriage nearly all of the money they spent was money that she had earned and not the money from his trust. Now that he wants to divorce her, being that they are in a community property state, they will split all of the assets that were earned during the marriage."

Irina looked confused. "I don't understand; it was her money."

"True. But as soon as they combined everything, there was no clear way of showing what was hers and what was his. My client's husband received money from his trust but it went directly into his bank account which was solely in his name. Whenever they spent money they always spent her money that was in their joint account. So now at the end of eight years she has almost no money left of her own investments. The house that they purchased with her money is in both of their names and most likely will be split down the middle. Not to mention that the house has decreased in value tremendously since they bought it. All the money that he received during the course of the marriage was never commingled and none of it was ever used to pay for any of the marital property or living expenses. They are still fighting over all the details but it looks like she will walk away with about a tenth of what she entered into the marriage with and he walks away with considerably more than what he started with and he still has his trust money!"

"That's absurd!" said Irina, clearly outraged. "I thought you said he was rich. Why is he taking her money?"

"He is rich. His family is worth over a billion dollars and he has multiple millions of dollars in his name but it was all in the trust prior to their marriage. The never discussed money and she was never included in the trust. All the money that was earned during the course of the marriage was earned by her. On top of that she stopped working so much because he promised he would always take care of her. I can't say that I blame her being that she was involved with such an affluent family. But because she didn't have a prenup and she generously commingled her funds, it's going to be a long process and a lot of it will be up to the judge. Since they're in a community property state it doesn't look good for her. Regardless, her once bright financial future is pretty bleak right now. She is starting over completely from scratch. She has less than $100,000 in her retirement account."

Irina sat there with her mouth open. It was clear that she had never considered these possibilities.

I spoke up at this point.

"Wow, Topaz, way to put a damper on things."

Topaz realized she was being a little too realistic for the occasion and started to say something when Irina cut her off.

"No. Thank you. I'm so glad I have a friend like you that knows this stuff. You're right, I hate thinking of the 'F word'," Irina does air quotes "but until this moment I never thought about money this way. I'll spend three months planning a four day vacation, hell, I will spend all week planning an outfit for a party, but I haven't given a second's thought to how to handle my finances after marriage. I'm sorry I was getting a little angry with you. I know you are just looking out for me."

"Irina, I'm sorry too. I tend to get very passionate about these things because I've seen such bad situations happen to people that could have been prevented. I really just want you to be happy."

"Awww. Do you think we can go over my finances sometime soon? I think I would rather talk to you first before bringing it up with David."

"Of course, darling, anytime."

"Good, I feel better knowing I am going to address this head on. I really don't like to talk about money."

"Me either." I agree. "The F word is a total downer. I hate thinking about my financial situation."

Eric appears with another server who begins clearing our plates.

"How was everything today ladies?

We all talk at once saying how wonderful the meal was and Irina says something to him in Russian. He listens to her carefully and nods his head in agreement.

"Can I bring you some espresso?"

I look to Topaz and she is looking at Irina. Irina is about to open her mouth to respond to Eric but instead looks down at her watch.

"Oh my gosh I didn't realize the time! I am supposed to meet David uptown in half an hour.

"Very well should I bring you your bill or would you two like to linger?" He said addressing Topaz and me.

Topaz looks at me and I shake my head no.

"Just bring us the bill. Thank you so much.

Once Eric left Irina says that we can take the limo and she will get a cab uptown. Topaz protests.

"Nonsense, we will just ride with you uptown and then take the limo back down to the building."

After we pay the bill and freshen our lipstick, the three of us headed out of the restaurant. The hostess handed each of us a small bag with a ribbon tied around it and a note card attached.

"Thank you so much for dining with us today we appreciate you choosing us for your celebration. Congratulations. This is from the pastry chef for you to enjoy later." She said indicating the gift bags.

We thank the hostess as we each took a bag and headed out the door. It was now early afternoon and the sun was bright overhead. The doorman and the driver opened our doors for us and we all got in. Once inside the limo I opened up the bag we had just received. Inside elegantly wrapped were several brightly colored macaroons. What a nice touch I thought. I closed the bag and begin to retie it again with the ribbon when I noticed the note card. Mine said "For Happiness" on it in a very nice handwriting.

"What does yours say?" I asked Irina and Topaz who were engaged in conversation about shoes again. They both looked into their bags and Topaz squeals with delight as she leans over to read Irina's note.

Irina holds her tag up. It says "To Love". How fitting, I thought. We all seem to have grab bags randomly but it was perfect her card said to love. I glanced over at Topaz's note and her says "Play More". She shows the note to Irina and the three of us all laugh together like it's a private joke. The last thing Topaz needs to do is play more, I thought.

A GIFT

We had a pleasant drive uptown to drop off Irina. David was waiting for her on the corner. Upon seeing him we all got out of the car to congratulate him.

Irina introduced Topaz and I to David. He was very polite and charming. We complimented him on his tastes in rings and, of course, remarked about how happy Irina is.

David was very gracious and warm to us. He remarked that with proposing to Irina not only will he be gaining a wife but two sisters.

I love the idea that he was automatically adopting us as family. Especially remembering that he is an only child and taking on not one but three additional women into his life would be quite an endeavor. I felt that spoke highly of his personality.

We got back into the car and gave the driver directions to go back to our building. Topaz and I talked a little bit about how cute of a couple Irina and David make and how happy they seem to be together. We then ran out of small talk and were silent for a few moments.

"I thought it was very interesting how you brought up planning for your future self."

"What do you mean?"

"I mean that you are right. We plan to go to the gym, we plan to go to a restaurant, we plan our outfits, we plan our vacation yet we really don't plan for our future from a financial perspective."

"Really? You are an attorney and I would think that of all professions yours would be the one that would be the most concerned about your financial future because you know of all the legal issues that can arise. We are such a litigious society that having all of your money tied up in a lawsuit is a very real possibility."

All at once I was embarrassed, frustrated, confused and a little bit angry. Where does Topaz get off saying that I should have done better I think to myself.

"Well, it's not that I'm not aware of all the potential issues that can happen. I mean while we live in a country where we are innocent until proven guilty that is not the case for money. Our money is usually considered guilty until proven innocent. I can think of numerous cases I studied in school where all assets were frozen while a trial went on. The simple accusation of wrongdoing was enough for the powers-that-be to tie up their funds. I know that if I was advising a client I would agree with you and have them set up a trust or at least get a prenup. But somehow I've never apply these principles to my own life."

Topaz is nodding her head in understanding.

"You're not alone. You know the old saying the shoemaker's children has no shoes? I see this frequently and I feel that many people go without the proper financial planning because they are reluctant to admit their true financial status. Often it is only the extremely wealthy that want to sit down with a financial planner. Which is fine I typically deal with very large estates and extremely wealthy clients. However I feel I would have a lot more of those types of clients if I were able to address these issues earlier on. Especially for women because they have so much more potential than men. I really feel that it is our time to shine. The number of successful women have been on the rise for the past several decades. I can give you example after example about how women have been rising to the top much quicker than their male counterparts. All you need to do is think about Oprah, Madonna, Angelina Jolie, Victoria Beckham or, for fuck's sake, even the Olsen twins. Who would have thought that such young women could have such an amazing, successful empire? It is because of their careful planning and strategies from the beginning that have made them the successes that they are. I would love to see that happen with every brilliant woman I come across."

"I have to admit, I have been feeling very empowered lately. I feel that there are far more opportunities for me today than there were just a few years ago."

"I absolutely agree with you. What's appalling to me is when I see successful women who have earned a considerable amount of money throughout their lifetime but never actually do anything with it beyond the simple 401K contributions that they participate in at work. Most women don't want to dabble in investments and they're not really risk takers. Well, at least traditionally that's how it has been. But now we see daredevils that are female and even if you look at Marvel or DC Comics you will see more and more strong female leads. Even Netflix has an entire category in action-adventure that show strong female leads. I don't think that you would have seen that 10 years ago. However all that being said those same women aren't looking at their finances the way a man would. Look at Irina, she is an extremely intelligent woman yet as soon as the man of her dreams comes into her life she was willing to leave her whole entire financial future up to fate."

No longer was I feeling frustrated or even angry. Topaz was making some very good points.

"That's all fine and good but I don't see myself having a huge increase in salary any time soon. As a corporate attorney I don't expect to be opening my own practice nor do I expect a giant bonus. In fact, just like my father, I expect to just be steadily increasing my income over the rest of my career. What choices do I have? My 401k is maxed and I have money in savings but I don't really know what else to do. I have never given any thought to retirement. I'm still waiting for the next phase of my life which is marriage."

"Why?"

"Why what? What do you mean?"

"Why? Why do you think marriage is the next phase? Why are you waiting?"

"Well, that's just because that's how it's always been done. You get married, have babies, raise the children, send them to college and then go into retirement."

As I am saying this I realize how outdated my thinking is and how things just don't necessarily happen like that anymore.

Topaz says "Yes, that is common thinking. However do you consider yourself typical in any way?"

I considered her question thinking of my cousins, school mates and the girls I grew up with and I shook my head no.

"I understand what you're saying but I wasn't really wanting to start planning my future because I feel like it hasn't started yet until I have found my mate."

Topaz is grinning at me nodding.

"That's fair. What's bad about that type of thinking is it puts us even further behind the curve. Statistically women earn less money than men doing the same job. If you factor in the time that most women take off to raise a family, it puts us even further behind. Let me give you an example: let's take a male and female that graduated college from the same school at the same time. To make math easy because I know it is not your favorite subject like it is mine –"

Jokingly, I interrupted her with an elbow in the ribs, "I do fine with math thank you very much."

"OK. I'm kidding but let's just make this easy. Let's pretend that each person was going to graduate from college at age 24 and for every year until the turned 30 they'd receive a 10% increase in salary. Are you with me?"

"Yes, I said." Suddenly unsure of just how good my math skills were without a calculator.

"OK. They both get the same job, working at the same firm. At 25 years old they both make $50,000."

"OK, I understand and so the next year they both would make $55,000 because of the 10% increase?"

"Exactly. So here's how it will go," Topaz does some math in her head. "Age 25: $50,000, Age 26: $55,000, Age 27: $60,500, Age 28: $66,500, Age 29 would be $73,000 something and Age 30 would bring them to like $80,500. My math is good but I will need a calculator to give you exact figures, but you get the idea, right?"

"Yes, I'm with you so far."

"That's in a perfect world. In reality, women earn about 80¢ on the dollar to men. While it varies by profession and the figure varies a bit, 80¢ on the dollar is a conservative estimate. "

Shaking my head.

"I know. We are closing the gender gap but I think it's going to be another generation or two until we're paid equally. So in your example even though the guy got the job for $50,000, the gal is only getting paid $40,000, right?"

"Yes. Exactly! It's a substantial difference. But let's just throw another factor into this equation – let's say that the female has two kids during that period of time. Undoubtedly she will need to take some time off for the pregnancy, delivery and maternity leave. Let's say she only works 80% as much as she would have otherwise. So now she is getting a 10% raise on less money."

About this time the driver pulls up to our building. He gets out and opens our door. We thank him and offer him money but Irina had pre-paid the bill. As we are walking up the steps, Topaz is punching numbers into her phone. Our doorman Roland is holding the door for us.

"Did you have a nice brunch?"

"Yes," I say, "Thank you so much. It sure is a beautiful day."

"Yes it is. I hope you enjoy the rest of it."

I thanked him and caught up with Topaz who was slowly walking ahead towards the elevator. She finishes and pulls me aside. We stood there in the alcove of our lobby as Topaz is shaking her head.

"I punched the actual figures into a spreadsheet real quick. It's worse that I thought. The first set of numbers shows how much each would make if both are receiving the same salary. The second set of numbers shows how much the woman would be making at 80¢ on the dollar. The third set of numbers shows if she were to only work 80% of the two for two years while she was pregnant/gave birth."

I looked at the tiny chart on the screen of her phone.

Age	25	26	27	28	29	30	Total
M	50,000	55,000	60,500	66,550	73,205	80,526	385,781
F	50,000	55,000	60,500	66,550	73,205	80,526	385,781
M	50,000	55,000	60,500	66,550	73,205	80,526	385,781
F	40,000	44,000	48,400	53,240	58,564	64,420	308,624
M	50,000	55,000	60,500	66,550	73,205	80,526	385,781
F	40,000	44,000	38,720	53,240	46,851	64,420	287,231

"Wow. I see what you mean. So not only do we earn less because we're taking time off to have babies but we also earn less because we actually earn less than men."

"Yes. We earn less and we live longer. Go figure!"

"That's just depressing."

"Nonsense. We live longer and we're smarter! We're lucky."

We both laughed. She had a good point. However I had reached my maximum financial discussions for the day; she had given me a lot to think about though.

Topaz and I walk to the elevator banks and she continues talking.

"I'm not trying to paint a doom and gloom picture. I am very optimistic about the future of women in business. Everywhere you look you see more and more success stories about women who started their own businesses or are taking over CXO positions in major companies. Pretty soon we will rule the world!"

We both laugh. I'm not sure if she is serious but I like the idea of women having more opportunities for success.

The elevator chimes to signal its arrival and we both stepped on and hit our respective floors. As the elevator ascends Topaz turns to me.

"If you would like my help, I would be happy to look over your finances. I promise not to bore you with math. I try to speak plainly and frankly to all of my clients and especially my friends. What I find that many wealth managers and financial advisors do is use so much technical financial jargon that no one actually understands what they're saying but other financial people. It creates an environment that leads to people feeling uncomfortable because they don't have a better understanding of what was just said. I believe the burden of explanation is on me rather than the burden of understanding being on you. No pressure. If you don't want to talk about your financial goals and how you are going to get income when you've retired it is fine. I would not be insulted at all but the offer is there and, of course, I will do it for free over a bottle of wine."

"Thanks" I said just as the elevator arrived at the 12th floor. We both air kissed each other and I stepped off the elevator onto my floor and began walking to my apartment. Retirement income? What did she mean about retirement income? I thought to myself then it dawned on me when I'm retired how am I going to pay my bills? Funny enough I had never really thought about the question that way. Everyone says Social Security won't be there by the time we retire. I have no idea if that's the case or not, I would have to figure that the government would have some sort of benefits program in place but who can say? I had no idea what my living expenses were going to be and I had no idea what the inflation would make my expenses. Now I begin to worry about what I would do when I stopped working.

When I walked into my apartment I realized that I was getting a little bit stressed about something I had never really thought about before. I guess if I'm talking to Topaz at least I know she won't think that I'm an idiot or make me feel embarrassed that I haven't done more planning. I am a little motified I haven't come up with any type of financial plan yet.

● ○ ● ○ ● ○ ●

I had spent about an hour in my apartment listening to music while cleaning the house. My phone buzzed and I went to check the text message:

> Just thinking about you. How was brunch? Do you have time for a walk? It is a beautiful day :-)

The text was from my boyfriend Greg. I probably have Topaz to thank for us meeting. Even though it was by chance, he had seen me many times before but it was only because of Topaz that he actually said hello to me. Well, actually she had given me some lotion with glitter in it and I was looking at the glitter in the sunlight when I bumped into him so she's kind of to blame. Greg has been really great and I have enjoyed our talks.

> That sounds great. I can be down in 5 minutes.

I texted Greg back. He lives only a few blocks away and we walk regularly along the water and have conversations and laugh. It's actually where we had our first kiss. Moments later I received another text from Greg.

> Perfect! I can't wait to see you. MUAH!

I laughed at that text. What guy texts MUAH? But it was really endearing. I freshen up my lipstick and comb my hair, grab my keys and I'm out the door.

By the time that I was down the elevator and through the lobby Greg was already outside my front entrance. He kissed me hello and told me how good I looked. I love the fact that he is always giving me compliments. He looked amazing also and he always smells so good.

"How was brunch?"

"It was really good. It's great to see Topaz."

"Where did you guys go? How was the food, did you have a Bloody —"

I cut Greg off mid-sentence.

"Irina got engaged!"

"Really? To who? I didn't know she was seeing anyone. You've never mentioned she was dating."

"Yes. It was a little bit of a surprise to me also. I knew she'd been seeing this guy who looked Israeli and I didn't know anything else besides that. It turns out his name is David and he is actually former Mossad. He proposed to her a couple of days ago and she waited until today to tell the two of us together."

"Well, that's great news. She deserves someone who makes her happy; she's such a nice girl."

"Yes, I agree. She is really fantastic. However the thing that she said afterwards got us into a whole new conversation at brunch which was very interesting."

"Why? What did she say?

"She said something like how she doesn't have to worry about money anymore because David is very successful and comes from a wealthy family."

"Hmmm."

"What do you mean 'Hmmm'?"

"She did not strike me as a gold digger. I am a little surprised at that comment."

"She isn't a gold-digger! Why would you say that?"

"If she's not concerned about her financial future because now she's married to someone who is financially secure what does that make her?"

"That makes her a woman! Men are supposed to take care of us."

I was immediately astonished that statement came out of my mouth. Greg stopped mid stride. He turns to look at me.

"If things between us get serious do you expect me to pay for all of your expenses?"

"Of course not! I make a good living and I can support myself."

"But you would expect me to handle all of our finances?"

"I don't know." I stammered, "I never thought about it."

"This is what I don't understand about women. They get all up in our business about what our finances are but when it comes time for us to ask the same thing they clam up. It almost always ends in tears. It's like you can't have a serious conversation about money with women. Why is that?"

"I have no idea. I never really thought about it like that. Tim was saying the same thing."

"What? That she needs to find a man that can support her?"

"No, that women need to be more willing to look at their financial situation. It turns out that she is a finance person. I didn't realize that's what she did for a living. She wants to talk to both of us about our financial future. She claims that once we have a financial plan it will give us the freedom to have a happier life.

"She's right. Your girl Tim always seems to have her shit together."

"You agree with her?"

"100%. Women never want to talk about money. I dated a girl that was an absolute disaster when it came to her spending habits. She would buy all sorts of clothes but then wouldn't have enough to pay her phone bill. It was really unattractive."

I thought about this for a minute. I didn't really like that he brought up his old girlfriend but I did like understanding the things that upset him. I was also surprised that he called not being fiscally responsible unattractive.

"I never really thought about finances when it comes to relationships because I've always just handled everything myself. I guess I thought that once I got married everything would magically be resolved."

Greg is looking at me like I have two heads. He's shaking his head in disbelief and starts speaking.

"How have you not thought about money and relationships? You're an attorney. You're a very smart and savvy woman. We have never talked about income, but I assume that you do very well for yourself."

"Thank you. I do OK. I didn't think that it was time for us to be discussing money."

"When is the right time to start talking about money?"

"I don't know I've never had a relationship get to the point we talked about it."

"Don't you think that that is something that is a major sticking point in any relationship? If you don't start talking about money in the beginning what happens if you get to the point where you're ready for the next step and the two of you disagree? And, let's back up a second, why haven't you talked to somebody about your financial plan? Creating a financial plan was one of the first things I did with my first job. Who is managing your 401k?"

"What do you mean who is managing it? I just put money into it with every paycheck."

"I am not a financial advisor but I think that's something you want to talk to Topaz or some other person about. Leaving your money in an account without ever actually looking at it is generally not a good idea."

"OK. Have you ever thought about retirement income?"

Greg looks at me with concern.

"Do you mean have I thought about how much money I will need in retirement and where that money is coming from?"

"Yes. It was something that Tim brought up."

"I take it that you have not determined how much you'll need or how you're going to receive income yet?"

"No. I'd never thought about it until today." I was feeling like I was a little slow. I am a very good planner in all areas of my life but never had given money much of a thought. I put money in my retirement account and I have plenty of savings. I thought that was all I was supposed to be doing.

Greg stopped and gave me a big hug.

"Don't worry. You have a lot of time but don't put it off either. Why don't you sit down and talk to Tim. Then you can talk to me about what she said. Heck, I didn't even realize she was in the financial industry. I may want to sit down and talk to her too. I have a financial advisor but because I'm not a very big client I'm not sure that he really reviews my account as closely as he would have if I had more money with him."

"I did not know until today that she was in the financial services business, I just knew it was something money related. For some reason what we did for a living never really came up. It never hurts to get a second opinion. Maybe what I could do is talk with her about my finances and then we can compare what are financial advisors told us."

"That sounds like a good idea when are you planning on sitting down with her?"

"She offered today but since she just got back in town I may give her a few days before sitting down with her. Just so she can get caught up."

"What is her fee? Do you know?"

"I believe her fee is a bottle of wine."

With this we both laughed.

"Sounds like you're getting off pretty cheap."

Freedom to Live Happy

THE F WORD

Greg and I had a nice walk and we continued talking about our weeks. It was always nice to have his opinion after Topaz hit me with some type of bombshell. Before she had left for Paris she had talked to me about her secret path of bliss. She claimed that by finding beauty in everything around her, celebrating it and appreciating it that it would create a more blissful life. I had put into practice some of the things that she had talked about and I have to say that my life has improved dramatically. I didn't realize how miserable I had been until I started waking up every morning with a big smile on my face.

Greg walked me back to my apartment and I went upstairs to relax a little bit. It was now nearly dinnertime and I wasn't sure what I was going to do this evening. I assumed that Topaz would be jet-lagged and Irina is probably still out celebrating her engagement. I may just call it an early night.

My house phone rings. Which was odd because I wasn't expecting anyone. I pick it up expecting to hear the doorman but instead it's Topaz.

"Mel, what are you doing?"

"I wasn't planning on doing anything. I figured you would need to adjust to the new time zone."

"Nonsense, darling. I hope you don't mind me calling. I asked the doorman to connect us, my phone is updating itself."

"Oh, no, that's no problem. What did you have in mind?"

"Well, I have been unpacking most of the day and I found the presents I bought for you and Irina. Do you want to come up to my apartment?"

"OK. But give me a little bit because I haven't had dinner yet."

"Melissa! Do you really think I would invite you to my apartment without giving you food?"

I thought about this and she's right every single time I came up to her apartment she's always had some type of goodies there for me.

"No, I guess you do always feed me." I said sheepishly.

"That's great! Irina is already on her way up. Come up as soon as you can."

I looked around my apartment anxiously wondering what I could bring with me. I need to keep a Topaz box so that when she gives these impromptu invitations I have something to bring with me. Alas, my sparse kitchen didn't have any items that I thought would make a suitable hostess gift so I went to the elevator empty handed.

I pressed the up button and waited for the elevator to arrive. When the bell chimed I got onto the elevator and wondered what Topaz got us while she was in Paris. I can only imagine. One of the first times I ever met her she baked edible glitter in my kitchen. Such a diverse person. As the elevator climbed to the top floor where Topaz's apartment was it stopped on 18. When the doors opened I saw Irina. She was wearing a cute champagne-colored jumper and gold stilettos. She looked amazing as usual.

When Irina saw me she shrieked with excitement. Hurriedly, she walked into the elevator and gave me a double air kiss. We both complimented each other on our outfits. I'm not sure why she complimented me on mine as I was just in yoga pants and a cute top I found at Victoria's Secret. But it did suit me and I was feeling pretty stylish even though I was casual.

The bell signaled the elevator was at the top floor and the doors opened. Irina and I walked to Topaz's apartment linked arm and arm. I felt better seeing Irina was empty-handed as well. I always felt funny about showing up at someone's house without a gift. But I suspect no one can anticipate having a gift at a moment's notice.

No sooner had we knocked on the door that Topaz opened it wide for us to come in. She greeted us with big smiles and air kisses. All three of us exchanged compliments back and forth about how fabulous we all were. Topaz was wearing cut off jean shorts and a chic T-shirt with something written in French. She was barefoot and there were open suitcases and clothes all over her bed.

Some delightful French song was playing through her speakers. It sounded like we were in a Paris café. Without even asking us she had already poured us flutes of champagne. I guess she already had it open. Topaz holds her glass up for a toast and we both do the same.

"Cin Cin!"

"Cin Cin" Irina and I repeat.

We all drink our champagne and it tasted amazing. Topaz has sliced apples, sliced pears, cheeses and meats already spread out on a tray. There's also an open box of crackers as well as some dips.

"Go ahead and help yourself. I have just been snacking all day."

You could tell Topaz was in a fantastic mood. Her apartment looked fresh and vibrant even though it had been basically closed up for the past six months. I had missed this place with all of the energy and ideas that had come from here.

"Come sit down," she says to Irina and me.

"Irina takes her stilettos off and sits cross-legged on the floor. I do the same and sat on the floor. It felt like the right thing to do in such a casual environment.

Topaz comes and sits down but is wearing sunglasses.

"What's with the sunglasses? Are they new?"

"I need them because your diamond is blinding me." says Topaz as she indicates Irina's gorgeous engagement ring.

Irina clearly enjoyed the attention and blushed.

"Oh stop it! I don't wear sunglasses in your apartment and everywhere you look there's bling. Have you gotten more gold trinkets?"

I looked around it did seem like she had gotten more golden items in the apartment. But it was hard to tell because there were things crammed in every space.

"You are just jealous," she says to Irina, jokingly.

Topaz is already topping off our flutes of champagne even though they are still basically full. I think Topaz has something against empty glasses. I don't think that I have ever been so well taken care of as when I'm in her presence.

"I have presents for you!" exclaims Topaz

"I can't wait to see what you got us!" says Irina.

Admittedly I am very curious too. I am wondering what fabulous Paris boutique was included in her shopping spree. I started to recount the famous designers that all got their start in the City of Lights.

Topaz excitedly gets up and walks across the room to one of her open suitcases. After tossing aside a few articles of clothing she finds two identical bags.

"I got these for you both. But after our talk today I think that they are even more useful than I had originally thought. Take a look!"

Topaz handed Irina and me each a bag. My bag was identical to Irina's. It was just a simple black shopping bag with a corded handle. There was no extravagant bow like her little presents in the past. I open the bag and looked inside and there were two small packages both wrapped in tissue paper. I opened up the bigger of the two first. As I unwrapped it I found a small bright blue leather book with an elastic ribbon keeping it closed. I took off the ribbon and opened the book and a 20€ Euro note fell into my lap. Europe has such colorful money. I briefly tried to remember if the Euro was more or less than the US dollar. I was pretty sure they were both the same, maybe Euro was like 10% more but really I never pay attention to these types of things. I opened up the blue book. It was blank. Questioningly I looked over to Irina who was also opening the book. Irina's book didn't have much in it either judging by the confused look on her face.

Maybe the next present would make more sense I thought. I opened up the other small box and inside was a pen. It was a metal alloy black pen; it was pretty but it wasn't necessarily fancy. I carefully sifted through the rest of the tissue paper to make sure I hadn't missed anything. I noticed that Irina was doing the exact same thing. When I confirm that these are the only items that are in the bag I put everything back into the bag except for the pen, paper and Euro note. I looked up at Topaz.

Topaz is grinning ear-to-ear. She is obviously very excited about the gift she has just given us. I'm not quite sure why she's so happy but I remember the lessons that I've learned from her to always be grateful and appreciate beauty no matter where we find it.

Irina beats me to it and stands up and gives Topaz a big hug.

"Thank you so much for thinking of me. It was so thoughtful of you to bring back something for us from your trip."

I get up and also give her as a hug and say thank you for the gift.

"You're welcome. But this isn't the gift."

Somewhat relieved I am happy because I wasn't really sure what to be doing with this little leather bound blue notebook. Much less the 20€ Euro note. You can never have enough pens but really I don't write that much so I'm not sure what the purpose of this gift was.

"Then what is the gift?"

"Well, as you know I was in Paris for almost six months for work. While I was there I was pretty much on expense account the entire time and you know how difficult it is to keep track of everything. I really hate doing expense reports. It was important to keep track of everything since I was being reimbursed for three meals a day and all of my daily expenses were reimbursed as well since my trip was extended for such a long period of time. They were covering a lot more expensive than your typical business trip."

I briefly wondered how much it costs to be in Paris per day. Topaz continued.

"I found these little ledgers in a store one day and as it turned out because of their size and that they were leather bound, it was easy to take everywhere. The elastic band holding it closed meant I was able to put little receipts inside without them falling out in the event that I was in a hurry and couldn't actually write things down in the right category."

I opened my book back up and realize that they were little categories. They were sectioned off equally but there was no writing on any of the tabs so I could make my own. I still don't understand why she gave us this gift though because I'm not on an expense account.

Irina says, "Well, thank you, again, for thinking of us this was very sweet. But you said you had another present for us?"

"Yes, my gift to you is a lesson I learned. I have always been very frugal with my money."

As Topaz made this statement I looked questioningly around her apartment. This did not seem like the apartment of someone who is frugal. Especially since she is on the top floor of our luxury doorman high rise building in downtown Manhattan. This was not a very inexpensive place to live. I have seen some of the clothes that she wears and there a lot of top name brands and beautiful designers. Plus we're always drinking champagne and one time we even had caviar. I think she must have a much different idea frugal than I do."

Topaz is looking at me and my face must have registered my skepticism.

"Melissa, I didn't say I live like a pauper. Let me explain."

Irina and I are both listening with rapt attention. We are both very curious as to how this book applies to us and what lesson Topaz learned.

"As I had to write everything down it gave me a better idea of my spending habits. I thought I was very much aware of my spending habits as it was. But now I started paying closer attention to how much I paid for absolutely everything. After a few days I learned some things; it was quite enlightening. For instance the small coffee vendor right outside of my hotel was almost double the price of the coffee vendor one block away. No surprise there because the vendor right next to the hotel has a better location. But I was passing the other vendor anyway and it didn't mean I couldn't wait an extra one minute for my coffee and save half the cost.

As I started writing down all the details of every single penny I spent what I realized that just by varying the times and locations of my purchases I could actually save a considerable amount of money. What I found actually quite funny was that now that I was accounting for all of my spending to someone else, actually didn't have a budget and could have spent more, I really ended up spending less. In fact my firm wanted to know what I did that I could keep my daily cost so much lower than some of my colleagues.

"Topaz, I don't understand what this has to do with us."

"I don't either."

"I got it for you so that you could spend one week writing down every single penny you spend. You don't need to write down your apartment and utility bills. That's something for later but I mean every purchase that you make. If you grab a salad at the deli, pick up a coffee at a bodega, buy a bagel, give a dollar to a homeless person, whatever it is, write it down. If you don't have time to write it down put the receipt inside the binder and as soon as you have a free moment enter it in. There are different categories and for me I chose to break it down as the following: food, needs, fun. I'm sure you can come up with better categories but I didn't have much space so I wanted to keep the word short. I used the word food for anything having to do with something I consume. If I wanted to get a mineral water on my way to work, if I was dining out or just picking up an apple from a fruit vendor I would put it all under food."

"Well does that apply like if you were going to buy groceries?"

"Yes, of course. We've already had the conversation about the different price of half a gallon of milk at that store down the street versus the one that's three blocks away. Remember I was telling you that the prices were so radical?"

"Yes, now that you had brought it up I always shop around when I'm buying my groceries. I now buy groceries almost every other day. So now I get my yogurt at one store and buy a chicken breast at another store. I have never looked at the actual prices of each individual item until you brought up the cost of milk."

"Exactly. My point is that most people don't know how much they spend on anything. So when you buy your groceries, you get home take a look at your receipt and actually pay attention to the cost of everything."

"I remember my friend was visiting from Ohio and kept complaining about the different cost of gas per gallon. She said that by her house the her gas was almost $0.50 a gallon more than it was by her office. She also noticed that on Mondays gas was the most expensive whereas on Fridays it could drop by $0.05 or $0.10 every single week. I had no idea that gas prices fluctuated that much based on location, day of the week and time of year. Since I don't own a car I never really pay attention to that but she says that now she only buys gas during the week by her office on Wednesdays that she saved about a dollar a gallon now because she combines it with one of her grocery store coupons."

"Exactly. It's about making the most of the money you have."

Irina clearly was not excited about the idea of writing all of her expenses down.

"This means I'm no longer going to be able to shop doesn't it?" Irina whined, suddenly looking very depressed.

Topaz looked at her sadly.

"Irina, for as long as you know me do you ever think that I would tell you that you couldn't go shopping?"

"No. But now you want me to talk about my finances and are wanting us to save money. The whole reason I work my butt off is so I can spend money on whatever the hell I want."

"And who is stopping you?"

"Well you wanted to write everything down so I guess I'm not going to be buying that new pair of Louboutin's I wanted."

"You didn't tell me about a new pair of Louboutin's which ones are they?"

"Don't try to change the topic. I saw these the other day and I was going to buy them this weekend. But I don't want to have to put that down."

"Why don't you want to write it down?"

"I don't know. They're almost $1,200 I don't want someone looking at that and saying I shouldn't have spent $1,200 on a pair of shoes."

"Why would someone say you shouldn't spend $1,200 on a pair of shoes? Do you have the money?"

"Of course I have the money. You know I got that new card the other day that has the reward points I was going to use that."

"No, I didn't ask if you could buy them I asked if you could afford to buy them. What about if I ask it like this? Can you go to the bank and withdraw all the money to purchase these shoes?"

Irina did some quick calculations in her head and then glanced down at her watch to check the date.

"I could but then I would need to put my rent on my credit card because I don't get paid till next Friday."

"So what you're saying is that if you were to pay cash for the shoes that it would put you in a bad spot financially."

"Yes, but who pays cash? I was just going to use my credit card."

"It is fine for you to use the credit card, especially if you're going to get reward points for your purchase that you can use for other things. But my question is if you had to pay cash for every single item that you purchase from now until the next 30 days would you still purchase the shoes?"

Irina sighed.

"No."

I'm pretty sure that Irina was starting to pout.

"Darling, I don't want you to not be able to enjoy your life but let's think about how extravagant you want to be. Why are you buying the shoes?

Are the shoes the ones that you're going to be wearing to your wedding? Or is this just the latest new style that you really want to have?"

"No, I have not looked for shoes for my wedding yet. I just really love the shoes and want to have them. And I don't think it is that much of a financial burden."

"I understand that. But how often are you falling in love with a pair of shoes that you absolutely must have? Is it once a month or is it four times a year? I only ask because if you break things down into a week-by-week basis if you buy a new pair of shoes like this once a month at a salary of around $100,000 per year after taxes that's almost three month's salary spent on shoes."

"What?"

"I said if you make $100,000 a year and you're basically taking out 25% for taxes that leaves you with $75,000 per year. Which divided by 52 comes out to around $1400 per week. Your shoes are $1200 plus tax, which is almost a week's salary. If you do that every month, you will have spent 12 week's salary on shoes."

I watched the color drain from Irina's face. I was glad I did not have the shoe fetish that Irina and Topaz seem to share. Noticing my smug look Topaz focused on me.

"The big items like shoes are the ones that are easy to pick out. The expenditures that I think of the most dangerous are the least expensive items that we purchase on a whim. I know I always see you walking home with magazines….."

I blink at Topaz wondering what magazines have to do with shoes. "Yeah, so?"

"Well, how many magazines do you buy per week?"

"I have no idea. I just pick them up. Basically on my way home like on a Friday night if I'm not doing anything. Or if there's a cover that I want to read."

"Why don't you get subscriptions?"

"Oh, I don't really want a subscription there are just some magazines that I want. I don't buy anything regularly." As soon as I said that I wondered if she'd noticed my stacks of US and People magazine at my apartment. I didn't even like admitting to purchasing them much less did I want a subscription.

"The last time you and I were together you had bought for magazines from a street vendor and the cost was nearly $60."

"It was not!"

"Yes it was, and you just handed him your credit card without breaking stride. I was shocked at the cost but assumed that you knew how much you were paying and didn't say anything."

As she said this I do remember purchasing those travel magazines. They were pretty pricey but at least I don't buy them very often. Suddenly I wondered if I was fooling myself, I seem to recall throwing out a huge stack of them just recently. Now I am wondering what other items that are in my regular routine of buying that I don't pay attention to because I'm not handing over cash."

"OK. I will make a deal with you two since you don't seem to be happy about my present to you."

We both look at her with some hope. I feel like this is when my trainer is telling me not to eat potato chips which I already know I'm not supposed to, but I like them so I still do. Oh, my trainer, I wonder if I need to list that in my ledger as well I thought absently.

"You have a choice. You can either put yourself on a budget for this week and pull out cash and pay everything with real money for the entire week or you can go cash free, use a credit card and write down every single item that you purchased in the ledger."

"Cash!" I say just as Irina says, "Ledger!"

As an afterthought Irina mutters "The B word is worse than the F word."

"What B word? Bitch?" I say.

"She means B for Budget. Irina, no budget, just keep track of your spending for the week. This will be a good exercise. Let's just do this for seven days starting tomorrow morning. How much of a budget do you want to have, Melissa?"

"For seven days?"

"Yes, just for seven days."

"And this doesn't include my rent or utilities or any of my normal bills, correct?"

"Correct."

"OK $100."

Topaz looks at me skeptically and shakes her head.

"Why don't we triple that?"

"$300? For the week? That's way too much money."

"Just because you have $300 does not mean you have to spend it. Personally I would have said $500 but will let you go with $300."

"Fine. But you will see, I will be much closer to $100 than $300. I really don't buy that much."

"That's great. It is wonderful to live simply like that."

"So I don't have to be on a B-word I just have to write everything down, right?" say Irina to Topaz, still pouting.

"Absolutely, just spend like you normally would and if you choose to buy any items that are not necessities make sure that the purchase won't interfere with any of your outstanding bills."

Irina seem to be content with this answer. I see her writing in her notepad already, I can see Irina written out in big bold letters from where I am sitting.

With that Topaz holds her glass of champagne up to toast.

"To Stilettos & Shopping!"

"To Stilettos & Shopping" Irina and I both coo.

This will be fun, I thought.

● ○ ● ○ ● ○ ●

The rest of the night we spent talking about Topaz's trip to Paris. It was great to have a girls night in. After listening to how passionate Topaz was about France, I decided I'd have to go very soon.

As the evening began to wind down Irina and I decided that it was time to say our goodbyes. We carry all of the dishes back to the kitchen and help Topaz clean up. While I'm standing in the doorway, it must have been the champagne speaking for me but with a dramatic gesture I do my best Romeo and Juliet.

"Parting is such sweet sorrow that I shall say good night till it be morrow."

Irina rolls her eyes and laughs.

"Not so fast, Missy" says Topaz.

I look at her inquisitively.

"Do you have your wallet with you?"

I had it with me but I couldn't imagine what she needed. Perhaps she hadn't exchanged all of her Euros for dollars yet and needed a little cash.

"Sure. What's up?"

Topaz held her hand out expectedly.

I look at her not understanding what she wants and begin to slowly open my wallet.

"All of your credit cards please."

"What do you need my credit cards for?

I trust Topaz, of course, but I'm not in the habit of leaving my credit cards with people. I'm a responsible adult and of course you have heard all of the stories about identity theft.

"Just keep your ATM card but I will take all the credit cards. You're on a budget remember?"

"Oh."

Woah. I guess this is really happening, I thought. I took a big deep breath and pulled out each card one by one and handed them to her.

"We don't want you to have any temptation, now do we?"

"Don't worry. I won't be tempted. I really don't spend that much money."

"Great. Tomorrow after you pull your $300 out of your bank account bring your ATM card to me too."

I felt like I was being challenged and my defenses were up.

"No problem." I shrug. "This will be a piece of cake."

However I felt like I had just given away some type of security blanket. Briefly I wondered what would happen in case there was an emergency. Maybe I should have one credit card just in case. But then that almost sounded like I was already admitting defeat so I just didn't say anything. Now Topaz turns to Irina who is smirking at my situation.

"I will take your ATM card please."

"What? Why do you need my ATM card I'm not on a budget." Irina argued.

"Actually, I will take your ATM card and every bit of cash you have on you."

"This isn't fair! I thought that I didn't have to have a budget."

"No, but you do have to have to be able to track every single penny you spend. So if you pay everything by credit card you won't have any option but to have a track of everything that you spent."

Irina looked wronged but reluctantly she hands over a wad of dollar bills and an ATM card. Topaz counts the money and then writes it down on a little Post-It note and hands it back to Irina.

Topaz turns back to me.

"Do you have any cash on you?"

"Of course, I always have some cash on me."

"Give that to me also," Topaz demanded. "Tomorrow you will start fresh with $300 and then we will reconvene in a week."

"OK. I think you're taking this a little bit far though. But I'll play your little game just to make you happy."

You could tell that Topaz was happy with my statement.

The next day I stopped at the ATM on the way into work and pulled out $300. Inwardly I rolled my eyes because I thought it was ridiculous to be taking out $300 when I know good and well that I only spend like $100 per week. But I took out the $300 just so I can prove to Topaz later this week that I didn't need all that money. I wasn't really sure what type of challenge she was trying to give me, I'm not the one spending $1,200 on a pair of shoes.

I thought about that and given the example that Topaz used with someone earning $100,000 per year the $1,200 pair of shoes was actually an entire week's worth of work. Knowing Irina and her constant wardrobe changes I wondered if she would even get an entire week's worth of wear out of the shoes.

I descended the stairs to get to the train and realized I needed a MetroCard. Remembering that I had to account for every penny I spent I briefly calculated what card I need it. Normally I just get the 7 Day card for $31 that gives me unlimited rides for a week but I generally only rode the subway 10 times a week so at a cost of $2.75 per ride it might actually be cheaper for me to pay per ride. Ridiculous I'm am spending time thinking about such a small amount, I thought. I handed the clerk two $20 bills and he handed me back my change and a 7 day MetroCard. I put my change into my purse and ran to catch my train.

When I was on the train I dutifully noted Subway $31 under Need. I just decided to use the categories that Topaz have used: Food, Need and Fun. I reasoned that if I had any business expenses I would just create another category called Biz. I was anxious to prove Topaz wrong about my spending habits because I know I have them very well under control.

Coming up from the subway stop near my office I stopped at my normal breakfast place. It's a combo bagel/newsstand. I order a regular coffee and bagel with cream cheese, he hands it to me and I pick up a People Magazine and an individual size bag of roasted almonds. I buy a People magazine almost every week depending on who is on the cover. I hand the clerk a $20 while still looking at the other magazines on display and he puts the change in my hand and hands me a bag with my purchase. Hurriedly I dump the change into my purse.

I catch an elevator just as it's about to close. I ride in silence up to my floor, humming a little tune to myself. Walking into my office there is already a flurry of activity. I unlocked the door to my office and have barely put my stuff down when my assistant asked me to stop by my boss's office. Hurriedly I grabbed a legal pad and pen and walk down the hall to his office.

"Melissa, I'm glad you are here. Do you have time to sit in on a meeting?"

"Sure, no problem."

My boss calls in two other people and they come in and we sit around his small conference table and discuss an impending matter. Afterwards he asked me to stay and we summarize some of the talking points of the meeting we just discussed. By the time that I walked out of his office it was a quarter past 11am. I finally sit down at my desk for the first time that day and suddenly remember my coffee. I pick it up hoping for some reason that it would still be hot. It's not, I taste it. Gross. I throw it out. I am about to eat the bagel when my phone rings. One of my direct reports is working on a very difficult case and asked if I would be free during lunch to discuss it. I agree. I hang up the phone, wakeup my workstation and quickly scan my inbox. I wanted to make sure there was no important pending matters. About 15 minutes later John walks into my office and knocks on the open door.

"Do you want to just go downstairs to the cafeteria and grab a bite to eat?"

"Sure, that's fine."

We talked briefly on the elevator ride on the way down to the cafeteria. I ordered my normal tuna fish sandwich, grab an apple, a granola bar and a mineral water. As the clerk is ringing me up John is continuing the conversation telling me how much he appreciates my open-door policy.

I hand a $20 bill to the clerk and she hands me back my change. I put it in my purse and carry my tray full of food to an empty table.

John and I discussed the problem he was having and work out all the points. When we finish we both carry our trays to the garbage and clean up our table. By the time I get back to my desk it's 1:30pm.

This day was flying by. I worked nonstop for the rest of the afternoon. I finally decided to call it a day around 8pm and headed home. On the subway ride home someone was carrying a bag full of food that smelled amazing. It was something Italian and I really started to get a craving for chicken parmesan. I recalled that deli on the way home had an amazing chicken parm and it was a good sized portion too. I thought I would go ahead and pick that up with a bottle of wine and then I would have dinner for both nights. I didn't go to the food store yesterday like I typically do but I will do that tomorrow after work on a full stomach. I know it's always better to shop when you're not hungry.

I stop at the deli and order a chicken parm to go and pick up an inexpensive bottle of Chianti. I stood in front of the counter, tapping my foot waiting impatiently for the food. As the delicious aromas hit me I realized how hungry I really was. While I was waiting I grabbed a Hershey bar and a small mineral water. The clerk rang everything up and it was $35.50! Taken back by the cost I asked how much the wine was assuming I read it wrong.

The clerk looks at the register receipt.

"$14.50."

"How much is the chicken parm?"

"$16.50" he says impatiently with a line forming behind me.

"Oh."

I hand him two $20 bills and he gives me back $4.50 in change which I dumped into my purse. When the coins drop into my purse I hear them clink against the other change that I had put in all day long and realized I hadn't entered in any of my expenses since putting the MetroCard purchase in this morning. No big deal, I thought to myself, after I eat I will write everything in. I know I have receipts for all my purchases.

By the time I walked up to my apartment I was famished. I opened up the bag with the chicken parmesan, uncorked the Chianti and poured myself a generous glass. It smelled scrumptious; my mouth was watering. I dished out half of the chicken parmesan onto a plate and carried the plate and glass of wine to the end table in front of my television. I watched TV as I ate. The chicken parm vanished very quickly. Briefly I considered eating the other half but bearing in mind the cost and that I didn't have any food in the house for tomorrow's dinner I chose to leave it for tomorrow. Remembering the Hershey bar that I bought I decided to have that for dessert and poured myself another glass of wine.

I only ate half the Hershey bar and I only drank about half the bottle of wine. I reasoned to myself that was great because I can just have the exact same meal tomorrow: problem solved. Now I got to my handbag and dumped it upside down to get out all my receipts to enter into my ledger.

First thing I did was straightened out all of the bills in my purse and then I grabbed all of the loose quarters at the bottom of the bag. I counted out the change, $20.50? I looked again. No, there was one $5, fourteen $1 and six quarters. That didn't seem right, I thought. I cringed. I must be missing something. I open my wallet to count the money that was still in there. To my dismay there were only nine $20 bills!

"That can't be right" I said to my empty apartment.

I picked up my handbag and dumped it upside down again. A wayward paper clip fell out but nothing else. All the other contents were already spread across my table. I then opened it and examined it as if perhaps something was hiding in a compartment somewhere. There was nothing; my handbag was completely empty.

I then went searching for the receipts and gathered them all together. Mentally I recounted my two "big" purchases: $31 for the MetroCard and $35.50 for dinner. Well Monday and Tuesday's dinner I said to myself trying to justify the purchase. I found the receipt for lunch. It was $17.75.

When I saw that I was suddenly relieved, obviously I was charged for my meal and John's. I examined the receipt closer so I would be able to determine what amount was mine and then what amount I should put under the Biz category for John's meal. But after reviewing the receipt I realize it is only for four items.

"My tuna fish sandwich was $11.25!? That's insane! It wasn't even that good." I yelled to my apartment walls.

I'm not sure why I am ranting like a lunatic. But it seemed like the right reaction. My tuna fish sandwich was $11.25, the mineral water was $3 and the Granola Bar was $2.25. The only thing that was reasonably priced was the apple which was a $1. Wow, I had no idea.

I looked for the receipt for breakfast. I know breakfast was not expensive. I find a receipt that looks like it's for breakfast but it says it's $15.25. I look at the date and it is marked for today. I must have been overcharged I thought. I looked at the receipt which doesn't have any descriptions listed just a bunch of numbers. There is a charge for a $1.50 which is probably the coffee, a charge for $2.75, one for $6 and one for $5. Perplexed I think back to what I bought. This must have been someone else's receipt. The $2.75 I guess is the bagel. I thought it was $1.25, oh, but I had cream cheese. OK. $2.75 makes sense. What else did I buy? Oh, yeah, the almonds and the magazine. That was $11? No way.

I get up and walk across the room and see last week's People magazine. It said the newsstand price was $4.99. So I guess they rounded up a penny. Wait, so does that mean I paid $6 for a small package of almonds? There couldn't have been more than 25 almonds in there. That's insane.

A little angry with myself I entered all these items into the food category with the exception of the People magazine which I listed under Fun and the MetroCard which I listed under Need. A little bit in shock I tallied up my expenses for the day which turned out to be $99.50. Now I am really glad that Topaz had insisted I take out the $300, at this rate I wouldn't make it until Wednesday. To add insult to injury I didn't even drink my coffee or eat my bagel. And I only had a few bites of the apple at lunch and threw the rest away.

Immediately I got up and went into my kitchen to look for something to pack for lunch. I used to bring a lunch to work nearly every day, but I have fallen out of the habit when I got my promotion. Briefly I consider just taking the other half of the chicken parm to lunch but I was planning on having that for dinner. I made a makeshift lunch of a couple of boiled eggs, some slices of cheese and an apple.

The next morning, I got up a few minutes early and made some hot tea and ate a boiled egg. The meal wasn't nearly as satisfying as a coffee and bagel but I just saved like $5 and considering I only had $200 to last me for the next six days, I was going to be much more conservative. I walked to the subway and got on my train, glad that I had purchased a 7-Day unlimited pass. The train ride went quickly and 20 minutes later I was coming up the steps of my building. I smugly walked past the bagel guy, even though I was starving and went to my building. On my way into the office I got a text from my trainer Colin.

> Don't forget. HIIT today. See you at 6:30pm! ☺

My trainer! I panicked. What is his rate again? I couldn't remember I usually pay him in bulk but I don't have any credit cards and I needed to pay him. I text him back.

> Oh. Sorry, something came up and I won't be able to make it.

Almost before I had finish typing my trainer is texting me immediately back.

> That's ok. Remember I will still have to charge you for the session because it's within the 24 hour window. Do you want to keep Thursday's appointment?

That's right, I thought, I forgot about the 24-hour policy. That makes sense, obviously people can't just schedule and reschedule at a whim. But if I was going to pay for it anyway I may as well do the session. So I texted back.

> The problem is I don't have any credit cards with me today. I only have cash. If you will accept a single payment I will keep tonight's appointment but please cancel Thursday

I walk slower staring at my phone awaiting his reply, and a few seconds later it pops up.

> I understand. My normal single session rate is $100, however because you have been buying in bulk you only pay me $65. If you want to just pay the $65 today and then next week pay me to the bulk rate that would be fine.

Disappointed I do remember him telling me I was getting a big discount because I was his regular client. At the time I thought that $65 per session was a really good deal for Manhattan. Now that $65 is about a third of all the money I have it seems very steep indeed.

> OK! Thanks. I will see you tonight at 6:30pm but please cancel my Thursday session.

I reach the lobby of my office building as I walk up to the elevator I hear my phone buzzing with a text message. I reach into my purse and pull out the phone. It's a response from Colin.

> Great! See you later.

Wow! I thought now I am down to $135 for 6 days. I briefly considered talking to Topaz about getting my ATM card back. Then I remembered I hadn't given it to her yet. The elevator dinged to let me know it had arrived on my floor and as I walked towards my office considered if I should pull out another $200 like the original $500 amount Topaz had said to begin with. I was very stubborn and was determined to make the $300 week work for me. Obviously if I only had $300 a week normally I wouldn't have a trainer but since I had to pay for the session anyway I decided to just go ahead and bite the bullet and pay him today.

Work flew by and around 5:30 was packing up to head home so that I can go to the gym. As I am about to walk out the door my boss yells from his office to me .

"Don't forget our early meeting tomorrow morning. the client is downtown so I will swing by in a car to pick you up."

"No problem, I will see you then."

"I will meet you at 7:30am."

"Sounds good. Good night."

As I rode the elevator down to the lobby I remembered I needed to pick up my dry cleaning. The suit I wanted to wear for tomorrow's meeting was still there from Friday. Inwardly I groaned wondering how much that bill is. It's just a suit and a blouse, if I remember correctly, so it shouldn't be that much, I thought to myself. On the way to gym I thought about how hungry I was mentally recounting the very few calories I consumed today since I didn't buy lunch. I totally forgot I was going to the gym straight from work. I was starving!

As I walked into my gym I realized I didn't have a water bottle either and grabbed one from the Kiosk. I grabbed the big one and asked how much it was. The perky clerk behind the counter happily announced it was $6. I put it back and grabbed the small one.

"That will be $2 today."

"Thanks." and I handed her two $1 bills and went to the locker rooms to change clothes. I took $65 from my wallet and carried it with me to the gym floor. When I saw my trainer I handed him the cash.

"I'm not used to getting cash! What happened?"

"Long story."

Sensing I didn't want to go into it he cheerfully said "Well, let's get to it."

Even though I was really tired because I hadn't eaten much I gave my workout my all considering I was paying over a dollar a minute for the session. Then I wondered if after all of my overtime and work I bring home with me if I make a dollar a minute when I'm working. I'm definitely in the wrong profession I thought jokingly. The workout took forever because I was so tired but I was glad that I had come. When we were finished it was back to the locker to get my things and go home.

On my way home I had almost forgotten about the dry cleaner. I walked past just as they were closing. I quickly ran in the door and fished out my ticket. The clerk pushed some numbers into the machine and the endless hanging clothes begin to roll around towards us. He punches something into the register and tells me it will be $40.

Forty fucking dollars? I think. This is outrageous. It was just dry cleaning, how could it cost that much? I angrily get two $20s out of my wallet and secretly vow never to come to this dry cleaner again. My clothes arrive and the man puts them on the rack in front of me. Reluctantly, I hand him the two $20s.

He looks at the bills and hands one back to me. "Four-TEEN," he says. He looks at my like I'm slow.

I took the $20 bill back. Oh. $14 for dry cleaning seems more reasonable, I think.

He hands me $6 in change and thanks me for coming. I thank him too and happily walk off feeling like $14 was a bargain. As I am walking with my dry cleaning in one hand and gym bag in the other I realize that Topaz is completely correct: I have no idea how much things cost. I'm so accustomed to handing my credit card over and then just paying it all at once at the end of the month. I wasn't sure if $14 or $40 was going to be the right amount for my dry cleaning. $40 seems excessive but now that I'm thinking about it maybe $14 is excessive too. I only used this dry cleaner because it was the closest one to the apartment.

I hate to admit it but Topaz's exercise it is actually a very good thing for me.

I get upstairs and didn't even bother putting my dry cleaning away until I put the chicken parmesan in to the microwave. I was absolutely famished. I could not wait to eat something. I saw the half bottle of wine and was happy that I would have that to look forward to when I got home from food shopping. I pulled out a pad of paper and a pen to write down all the things that I needed at the grocery store. Luckily I shop every few days so it should not be that expensive. Then I recalled that I would need to be eating breakfast and lunch and dinner at home for the rest of the week so I got to thinking about what foods that I want to eat for the next 5 days.

While eating my dinner I thought of foods that would not be that expensive. Briefly I thought maybe I should just buy a whole bunch of ramen noodle like I had in college but then I reasoned I am a successful well paid attorney, my days of eating ramen should be over. I decided to just get some chicken, lots of vegetables and fruits. I can't imagine those items would be very expensive. After I finish eating and made my list I got ready to go to the store. Beforehand I needed to find out how much money I had left. I was a little bit concerned since this was only Day 2 of Day 7.

Once again I find myself dumping my handbag upside down onto the table. I am looking through all the ones and coins and counting all the money I have left. I kept searching through my purse in the event that there was some extra money magically stashed somewhere. Unfortunately there was not and the amount I had left was $119.50. I hope that would be enough to buy groceries. I wasn't really sure.

I walk to the grocery store with much trepidation. I was really feeling very stressed out about the amount of money I had remaining. I tried to anticipate what costs I would be having for the rest of the work week. Since my boss would be picking me up in the car I would not need to pay for the subway. It looks like it wasn't that smart of a thing for me to get an unlimited pass because I will probably only be getting on the subway 9 times this week which if I paid per ride it would have saved some money. I can't believe I was stressing out over $4 or $5 that I would have saved by buying a pay-per-ride card instead of the unlimited. I shook my head.

In the store, I grabbed a small cart and went down the tiny crowded aisle looking for the items that were on my list. Before I put anything in my cart I looked at the price. I was about to pick up some cheese when I realized that it was $26 per pound. I looked at it to see if it was encased in gold or something and put it back and picked up some Munster cheese. I quickly looked at the price on that package and it was only $5.99 a pound and this slice came to $3.21. No problem I can deal with that, I thought. I got everything on my list and looked in my basket, it didn't seem all that full. But still I was extremely stressed out about the clerk ringing it all up.

The store wasn't very crowded and I unloaded my few items quickly. The clerk raked each item across the scanner so fast I couldn't keep up But was relieved when I saw the total: $84.50.

FASHION

The rest of the week flew by, although it was not a great week. I was very stressed about money all week and held on to the remaining $35 I had in the event that something happened. I ate breakfast lunch and dinner at home. Well, let me rephrase that, I made lunch at home and ate it at the office. This made me very stressed out and much less social. Some of my direct reports asked if I was OK.

On Friday night as I was walking out of the office my secretary invited me to join them at happy hour. As long as I have worked at this company I've never ever been invited to a happy hour. Unfortunately I felt that I had to decline but I was uncomfortable saying why. I was very disappointed as there aren't many spontaneous opportunities to socialize casually with people that report to you. I very much regretted creating a $300 budget for me this week but it was definitely a learning opportunity.

"It really is a B-word," I muttered to myself.

Friday night Greg invited me out to dinner on Saturday night which I declined. I didn't like the idea of going out to a nice place to eat if I couldn't afford it and I couldn't think of any place in Manhattan on a Saturday night that we would be having dinner at that would cost less than $35. Greg sounded very hurt by me turning him down. I countered with an invitation to go for a walk Saturday afternoon. Unfortunately Greg had other plans that afternoon which is why he wanted to see me for dinner. We hung up the phone and I was a little stressed out. I could tell he seemed a bit distant.

Saturday I normally get a manicure and sometimes a pedicure but this week I did not. For the life of me I have no idea how much I paid for a manicure or pedicure and I didn't want to spend the money. My grocery supply had dwindled much quicker than I thought. I know I have lost weight this week because my skirt nearly fell off at work today. Being on a budget definitely requires a lot of work. It made the week very long. I went to bed early and realized this is the first Saturday I didn't actually have any plans. I decided I would just clean my apartment and go to the gym.

The next day as I was coming back from the gym I ran into Irina in the lobby. She seemed to be her normal bubbly self with her bright pink hair somehow appearing even more bright than normal. She gave me air kisses and could not have been more jubilant.

"Darling, it's so great to see you!"

"It's wonderful to see you as well. How has your week been?"

For the next 5 minutes Irina detailed all the things that she had done this week. She definitely had a very full social calendar and was in a fabulous mood. She looked great and briefly I wondered if maybe she'd had an injection or Botox on her face. It was somehow more vibrant than usual.

I listened closely and then asked "How are you doing with the Ledger?"

"Oh, I haven't entered anything into it yet I've just been stuffing the receipts into it and I'll do it all at once tomorrow morning before we meet with Tim."

No wonder she is in a good mood, I thought. She hasn't been on a budget.

"Do you know what time we are meeting Topaz?"

"She said 1pm."

"OK."

Irina looked at her watch and said, "Oh my goodness, I'm supposed to meet someone in an hour and I need to change clothes. Do you want to get drinks tonight?"

"I would love to but remember I'm on a budget? I can't."

"Nonsense, darling, I will pay; it will be my treat."

"Oh I couldn't do that. I don't think that's how this experiment is supposed to work."

Irina pauses for a moment and thinks. She realizes that I am probably right and tells me that after this week is over we will definitely go out for drinks. I agree and continue walking to go get my mail.

● ○ ● ○ ● ○ ●

That night as I stayed in my apartment, I realized that I could have been out with Greg having a good time. He makes me so happy and he's such a sweetheart I really regret not having the money to be able to go out. This has been one of the most stressful weeks I've had in a very long time. I read through my People magazine for about the hundredth time since it is about my only source of entertainment and decide that I will go to bed early once again.

I woke up early and had a headache. I went to the kitchen and look through the refrigerator but there was nothing in it but some condiments. I opened the kitchen cabinets and tried to imagine something that would be worth while eating. All I had was olives, pickles and a jar of tomato paste. I was afraid to go back to the grocery store since I only had that $35 left. However the good news was that it was only today that I had left.

"Fuck it." I said to the empty kitchen.

I closed all the cupboard doors and moved to my bedroom to put on some clothes to go outside. With much resolve I grabbed my wallet, put on some lip gloss and headed outside. I impatiently waited for the elevator to arrive and after a few minutes gave up and headed towards the stairwell. I took the 12 flights down very quickly and reached the lobby. It was 8am and it was a very busy Sunday morning. I walked right past the doorman and into the outdoors. Walking across the street I made a beeline for the bagel guy. To be honest I really did not care if a bagel and coffee cost me $35 I was famished.

When I got to the bagel cart there were a few people in front of me. While I was standing there for the very first time I noticed that there was a menu attached to the bagel cart, it's like I'd never seen it before. I don't mean that I've never seen a menu but this is the first time I've ever noticed a menu with prices. I quickly scanned down a coffee is $1 and notice the bagel is $1 as well! I can handle $2 but then I see the bagel with cream cheese is $2 which is much more reasonable than the place by my office. I looked around and the sparsely populated area the bagel cart was parked in was probably not the best place for his business. This area is not very busy on the weekends.

When it was my turn I ordered a regular coffee and a bagel with cream cheese. He efficiently handed both items back to me in a sack and requested $3. I handed him three $1 bills and walked off with my breakfast. I sat down on the first bench I saw and had a bite of the bagel.

"Oh my gosh" I said out loud.

Not having indulged in a bagel all week my mouth was watering. Then I took a sip of the coffee and it was delicious. I felt like Magellan or some other famous pioneer. I wanted to tell every person I know to buy their bagel and coffee from this guy. How much was my bagel and coffee by my office? I thought to myself. Wasn't it like $4.25? I then thought what if I had just bought coffee and a bagel from this guy and bought a big tub of cream cheese and left it in the office fridge. That would make the price $2 instead of $4.25, of course I don't know how much a tub of cream cheese is and leaving it at the office in the fridge seems kind of gross. I ruled out that idea.

I pulled out my phone and brought the calculator app open I punched in 4.25 x 20 = 85, it read. I further added 12 and press the multiplication symbol and it read 1020. Wow! I spend $1,020 a year on bagels and coffee. I then repeated the same formula substituting 4.25 for 3 and the result was 720. I stared at the screen for a minute and started thinking. Certain that I had done the math incorrectly I repeated the whole exercise. I realized that there were probably more than 20 working days in a month but it seemed like a good average. Plus I don't buy a bagel and coffee every single day sometimes I have meetings beforehand but according to my calculations it looks like if I spent $4.25 every working day at the office for 12 months I spend over $1,000 a year on bagels and coffee. Conversely if I bought the coffee and bagel here for $3 and carried it to work it would have cost me $700 a year. Quickly I punched a whole bunch of different numbers into my calculator app. If I skip the coffee or skip the cream cheese and the cost was only $2 per day it would cost me $420 per year. That's a much more manageable number than $1,020 I thought to myself. I smiled having virtually just saved myself $600 annually.

As I got up from the bench and walked back to my building I felt really satisfied. Caffeine, carbs and fat, I thought to myself how can you go wrong? I went back to my apartment and lay down on the sofa to watch TV. Basically I was just killing time until going to Topaz's apartment at 1pm.

Wait! Topaz's apartment! This is my moment to shine I thought leaping from my couch. I quickly grabbed my wallet with the remaining $32 in it and headed to the liquor store. Last time I showed up at her house empty handed and this time I wanted to arrive with a bottle of wine. Why not? I can splurge, I have $32 left. I practically skipped to the liquor store and headed directly to the wine section. I still don't know much about wine but I went to the French section and found something that looks like a type of wine I thought she would like. It was $18. Perfect. I grabbed it and took it to the clerk.

"Do you want it gift wrapped?" he asked

"How much does that cost?" Realizing that I've never asked that before. It's a bit embarrassing how frivolous I have been without even knowing it I thought to myself.

"Oh, it's free. What color ribbon?" and he points over his shoulder.

Excitedly I spot a hot pink ribbon and a gold foil bag. "Can you put it in a gold foil bag with the hot pink ribbon?"

"No problem."

Seconds later I am walking out with an expertly tied hot pink bow and heading back to my apartment. When I walk into the lobby I glanced at my watch and it's actually 5 minutes after 1pm. I didn't realize the time. I went directly to Topaz's apartment on the 36th floor and knocked on the door.

A few minutes later the door opens and I can hear hysterics in the other room. Topaz opens the door and greets me with a concerned look on her face. She's not her normal cheerful self. I can sense a different vibe in the apartment, once I walk inside I can see Irina looking distraught, her face blotchy and red. You can tell she had been crying. Topaz is handing her a box of tissues. Irina looks up to me and puts on her best face.

"Hello, Darling, you look amazing."

"Hi, what's wrong?"

Fearing the worst I could only imagine what crisis had happened to Irina. I had never seen her so upset. I wondered if David and her had broken up or if it was something worse like a death in the family or some other tragedy. I walked over to sit next to Irina.

As I sit down I realized I was still holding the bag of wine. I held it up to eye level.

"Oh, I brought you this..." I said in a hushed voice to Topaz.

Topaz greedily takes it excitedly opening the bag. She is clearly thrilled with the gold foil and hot pink ribbon I picked out, this made me grin. She stands up and walks over to me and give me a big hug. If she's this excited about the decor I'm hoping that I did OK with the wine too.

Topaz goes into the kitchen to get a pair of scissors and gingerly cut the bag open. I heard her enthusiastically gasp from the other room. For a second I was worried that there was maybe a mouse in the apartment by the volume of the noise she made.

"You are absolutely psychic how did you do this?"

Remembering the last time I brought her wine it had been one of her favorite and she had actually been to that very vineyard in France. I wondered if I had done the exact same thing.

I look around the corner curiously and Topaz is coming in with a bottle of wine that's already opened and a glass. The bottle was about three-quarters of the way empty already. She hands me a full glass and displays the open bottle for me. I look at it wondering what it is that I'm supposed to see. Irina started laughing.

"You did it again!"

"I know she did. I can't believe it!" says Topaz

"What did I do?"

"Irina and I were just saying how we would need to go get another bottle of wine and you brought the exact same bottle we were already drinking."

"So I did good?" I grinned.

Irina leans over to me and gives me a hug. "You did fabulous, Mel."

Topaz thanks me again and put my bottle of wine in the refrigerator and comes to sit back down. I am still wondering what is wrong with Irina and don't really want to bring it up in case it makes her start crying again. Topaz sits down and lifts her glass up for a toast

"To living happy" she says.

"To living happy!" I toast to her and wonder about that statement because this week was not very happy for me at all and obviously something is going on with Irina. But Irina also raises her glass of wine. She clinks our glasses and also toasted "Living happy!"

We all take a sip of our respective glasses and Topaz begins to talk.

"I guess since you are bringing a bottle of wine you did OK this week with your budget?" Topaz inquires.

Uneasily I answer, "I did OK, but it wasn't any fun. "

"It wasn't supposed to be fun. It was just a learning experience" says Topaz. "How much did you end up with?"

I opened my wallet and pulled out two $5 and four $1 bills. "$14. I would have had $32 but the wine was $18."

Topaz covers her mouth and gets up and walks into the kitchen. She brings the bottle I brought and compared it to the one she had; they looked identical. She didn't say anything.

"What's wrong?"

"Nothing. So how was this week?"

This was the moment I had been dreading. I took a deep breath and told her about the whole week. I explained how I blew 100 bucks the very first day and how I was freaking out the rest of the week because of my trainer, the dry cleaning and I even had to turn down drinks with my direct reports because I was afraid of running out of money. I admitted I hadn't spent any money since Tuesday until today and it was only because I was starving.

I finished my story and realized that her and Irina were listening to me very carefully. When I stopped they both started laughing hysterically. I couldn't imagine what they were laughing about and was a little irritated.

"I feel so much better!" exclaims Irina.

"Why? What did I say?"

"You don't understand. You were on a budget and you were struggling. I was not on the budget and spending money the way I normally do. This morning when I added everything up I was horrified. I looked at her wondering how bad it was but I did not want to ask because I thought that was very personal. Topaz cured my curiosity

"Eleven fucking hundred dollars!" Topaz blurts out.

My jaw dropped. "$1,100?" I repeated, certain I had heard wrong.

Irina is nodding in agreement while looking very embarrassed.

"How?" I asked.

"Well, you know how you were shocked on that first day where you didn't really buy anything of interest? You just had breakfast, lunch and dinner like you always would. It wasn't anything extravagant but you still spent $100?"

"Yeah."

"I wasn't writing anything down until today. If I had done that, like you did on Monday, maybe I would have realized that I had spent $150, but I didn't. Then on Wednesday night I went out with a friend of mine to dinner at a very nice restaurant; I spent $300 there. Then we went to a club, that was another $80. I stopped into Bloomingdale's to pick up new shade of lipstick and while I was there I also got an eyeliner. Somehow that was $80.00. Basically every single day I averaged around $150, I had no idea I spent that kind of money. No wonder I don't have much savings."

Irina digs in her purse and handed me her ledger. I open my wallet and pulled mine out. The two of us compared each other's weeks. Well she was just having a normal, while slightly extravagant week, I was very grateful that I've had the budget of $300 even though I wasn't having a good time. We looked over the other's ledgers while sipping wine in silence. Both of us finished and handed our ledgers back to each other.

Irina turns to Topaz with a little tear in her eye and says, "Thank you so much for making us do this. I am so happy to get a better understanding of my spending habits. I think if I were to put myself on a budget, not as strict as Melissa's, but if I had like $400 per week and changed going out to a nice dinner only once a month I think I could still be very happy but I would have so much more money in the bank."

"I know. I am definitely making some changes because of this. Did you know that the bagel guy outside is like $2 for a coffee and a bagel and it's like twice as much by me at my office?"

Topaz's laughing and nodding in her head.

"Remember how we talked about our secret path to Bliss? Where if you are constantly grateful that you will have more things to be grateful for?"

We both nodded. That's how I met Topaz to begin with. Topaz had talked about the importance of appreciating the beauty that surrounds us and being grateful for all of it. Just by allowing yourself to really enjoy the pleasures in your life and taking in every wonderful thing around you that you can live a more blissful life." Topaz continued.

"Once you start paying attention to the cost of every item you will notice how much things should cost. Melissa, I sincerely doubt you will ever order a coffee and a bagel with cream cheese again without looking at the cost now that you know that it should be around $3 you would not pay $4.75 if you could avoid it. It's like the wine that you brought you said you paid $18 and I appreciate the wine. In fact, I know exactly where you bought it but if you had walked around the corner to the other liquor store on the other side of the street this same bottle is selling for $12."

"Oh! I didn't know." I defended myself.

"Of course you didn't!" Topaz says to me kindly with her hand on my arm. "Every purchase will be a learning experience. You wouldn't go out and buy a car without doing research to see if it was expensive to own or maintain would you?"

"I wouldn't buy a car."

We all laugh. Manhattan may be expensive to live in but not needing a car was a fantastic perk.

"OK that was a bad example but you know what I mean. You are going to do research on things you don't know about. Now that you know a coffee and bagel can be $2 you're going to be able to do a comparison whenever you're somewhere else. Who knows you could be in the Midwest somewhere and a coffee and bagel might only be a dollar."

"Since when do they have bagels in the Midwest?" asks Irina jokingly.

"You know the Midwest like Jersey." says Topaz laughing. "I am not doing very good with the examples but you get the idea. Kinda like how everyone knows if you rent a car and you go to New Jersey, you always fill up before you cross the tunnel because the prices are like 50¢ cheaper per gallon than in the City."

We both nod.

"I have a great idea" says Topaz as she pours us more wine.

"Oh no, not another great idea." Irina says faking a groan.

We all laugh.

"I have somebody I want you to meet. How about we all get cleaned up and meet for tapas at that place down the street around 4 pm?"

"I'm broke" pouts Irina.

"I only have $14" I chime in.

"Don't worry girls. It's my treat. Wait until you meet my new friend Francesca, I met her in a Muay Thai class. She's amazing."

We agree to let Topaz treat. I hadn't eaten a decent meal since Tuesday night's leftover chicken parmesan. I have numerous talents but cooking isn't one of them. We finished off the wine and Irina and I head to the elevator to go down to our apartments to get ready.

● ○ ● ○ ● ○ ●

As we ride the elevator down in silence each to their own thoughts I briefly wonder who this Francesca chick is. I know if Topaz likes her, she's either a lost cause like I was or she is a super vibrant person like Irina is when she isn't crying over her spending habits. Either way the more the merrier. I can't imagine Topaz hanging out with a negative person.

I walked into my apartment and decided to take another shower. Somehow talking about money just made me feel dirty. I am not sure why I have an aversion to planning my finances. That has been puzzling me all week. It really makes no sense at all but when Irina told us about her engagement and stated that she would no longer have to worry about money because she was marrying a wealthy man I thought that was a little outdated. But how was I any different? I make good money also but I haven't made a plan because I was waiting for the next phase of my life to start. I don't know what I was thinking because I would have to do the financial planning at some point. And, as a bonus, it might make me an even more attractive mate if I do have my financial plan in order. One thing I know for sure is after spending this week really scrutinizing my spending habits it made me realize I would like to make some changes in my life. Even if I don't do anything else differently and I just purchased my bagel from the guy down the street instead of the one by my office then I will already be saving a couple hundred bucks a year. All I need to do is make a whole bunch of little changes like that and it all adds up. I mean think about it this way, I paid for unlimited trips on the subway but as it turned out I only rode it nine times this week which means I "wasted" $6.25 with the unlimited MetroCard. Granted that's not really something that by consciously thinking about I can change. Most weeks I do ride the train more frequently. I guess what I could do is keep track of how many times I ride the subway for a month and just see what the average is. I feel like if I scrutinize my spending habits a lot more carefully I will end up with a lot more money in my bank account. That would be a good thing!

After my shower I went to my closet to look for a tapas-appropriate outfit. Topaz and Irina always look great and I really wanted to wear something fashionable. Besides who is this Francesca girl? She sounded exotic.

I ended up wearing cute sandals, tan shorts and a bright orange blouse my mom bought me. I added some accessories that felt very out of place but I knew they looked good. It was nearly 4pm so I walked out of my apartment to head to the elevator.

When I got to the lobby I looked around and didn't see Topaz or Irina. I hovered around the elevator banks waiting for the two of them to show up. Down the long hall at the other end of the lobby I see a girl at the front talking to one of the doorman. She is fairly petite and I don't think I'd ever seen her before. I wonder if that's Francesca? I thought to myself because I wasn't sure where we were meeting her. The girl looked fairly young so it probably wasn't her I reasoned, no one names their child Francesca anymore.

One of the elevators dinged to announce its arrival and once the doors open it revealed Irina and Topaz inside. They were already laughing and talking. Any trace Irina had been tearful earlier had completely disappeared. The two of them looked like fashion models and I'm now self-conscious that I'm wearing flats because the two of them were both sporting gorgeous stilettos. Irina and Topaz both give me air kisses and say hello telling me how amazing I looked and I did the same. About this time Topaz spots the girl at the other end of the lobby and yells across the long marble hallway "Francesca!"

The girl turns and looks at Topaz and heads in our direction as we walk towards the front entrance. Topaz walked up to Francesca and they give each other a big high-five. I thought that was a little odd because Topaz always gives me a double air kiss but then I remembered they met at Muay Thai kickboxing class so maybe this is how they greet one another in class.

Francesca is compact. Up close you wouldn't really call her petite because there is nothing frail about her. I'm not sure what it is but she seems to have a lot of strength in a small package. She's about 5'4 and probably not much more than a 110lbs, short, jet black hair in a pseudo-punk-rocker cut with big dark brown eyes. She has the underlying energy though like if a Pixie was a UFC fighter, that's how I think they'd look. I look at her outfit, relieved; she is also wearing flats with very ripped jeans and a tiny tank top revealing a serious set of abs. Topaz towers over her by at least by 6-7 inches with her crazy high stilettos. She turns to Irene and I.

"Ladies, I'm delighted to present Francesca! That's Irina and Melissa." She says pointing to the two of us. Francesca steps forward and sticks her hand out to me.

"Francesca Kahn. Nice to meet you." She says practically crushing my hand.

"Melissa Scarpetti," I say trying not to wince. "Caan, like James?"

"As in Genghis." she says with a clever smile.

"Irina Petrovia." says Irina, also shaking Francesca's hand.

"You can call me Fran-K, if you want. That's what my friends called me in LA."

"Fran K?" I said and turn to Topaz, "Tim, why does everyone have a nickname but me?"

Francesca turns to Topaz and asks "Tim?"

"T.I.M. My initials: Topaz Indigo Morgan," she says to clarify "Everyone always looks at me like I'm a stripper when I tell them my name is Topaz, so I just go by Tim a lot."

Fran-K starts laughing, "Promise you won't call me by my initials."

Irina says "Why what are your initials?"

"My middle name is Ultima." and doesn't say anything else while we spell it out for ourselves.

"Only if you get on my bad side." says Topaz while winking, "Are we ready to head out?"

We all nod in agreement and pair up to walk down the rest of the hallway and down the flight of stairs. The tapas place that Topaz had mentioned was only a couple of blocks away which left the four of us making small talk on the walk there. When we arrived at the tapas place surprisingly it was not very busy at all. But then again it was 4 pm on a Sunday so I guess there's not a lot going on right now.

The hostess sits us at a spacious table, well spacious for New York City, when I say spacious I mean the next table over won't elbow me if they pick up their fork. Topaz orders a bottle of mineral water and we all get bar glasses while looking at the menu. Typically when I look at a menu I'll look at the foods they have and not the price of the item but this time I went to the prices first . This was a pretty expensive restaurant I thought to myself none of the entrees were under $20 a piece. I may have to think about learning how to cook better because eating out all the time definitely cost me a lot of money. About this time the server shows up with a giant pitcher of sangria.

Eyeing Francesca suspiciously she ask her for her ID. Fran-K was already prepared with it so apparently she gets carded all the time. I looked at her wondering how much older than 21 she actually was. The server hands it back and she says "I assume you ladies are here for happy hour?"

I look up to her with a question in my eyes.

Confused the server looks down at the table and says to herself "I forgot the Happy Hour menus" and walked over to the hostess station to grab them and came right back.

"Here you go, I'll give you a minute. Help yourselves to the sangria, the first pitcher is included."

Included? I thought since when do they include alcohol? I open up the happy hour menu and suddenly all the prices were considerably cheaper. There were numerous items listed under small plates that were only $4 and $5. This was great, I thought.

The four of us reviewed the menu and discussed various possibilities. In the end we just decided to get a whole bunch of items to try everything on the menu. Once we finished ordering and made our first toast Topaz started to talk.

"Francesca just moved into our building."

"Really? Welcome to the building! I thought you two met at Muay Thai class."

"We did." said Fran-K

"Yes and then we both walked home and I thought she was following me. I even ducked into an alleyway in case she was about to attack me. I was ready to use some of my self-defensive moves on her."

"I thought you were a mugger!"

"Yes, I nearly got sprayed with mace."

"Pepper spray." Fran-K corrected

"Same difference." says Irina

"No, that's not true," says Topaz. "Mace doesn't work very well on people who are drunk or drugged up, it's like tear gas. Pepper spray is an inflammatory and will work immediately, unless they're like SpecOps or a superhero."

"I didn't know that" says Fran-K

"Me either." I said.

"Anyway, after that we became friends. As it turns out she lives on the same floor as me."

Topaz lives on the top floor and I wondered how this 20-something could afford an apartment with that type of view.

"Really?" I said to Fran-K. "You moved here from LA?"

"Yeah, I always wanted to live in NYC. I actually moved here for a job."

Topaz bursts into the conservation and says excitedly, "She's the head social media marketing director for a certain energy drink we all know and love."

Fran-K laughed. "Something like that, I have to keep it on the DL right now because we are about to explode with a new brand. They paid for my move and are covering my rent. Bump in salary too."

"Your job pays for a $4,000 a month penthouse level apartment?" Irina asks incredulously.

"Oh, no they only pay for $2,000 a month rent and I'm covering the rest. I figure why not? I've got the money."

Irina looks at me and we both look at Topaz wondering what she's going to say about that statement.

"What do you mean? You've got the money?" asks Irina.

"Well, I make decent money and they're giving me a $2,000 a month rent allowance so I just use the other two grand to make up the difference for the apartment. I really liked living in this building."

"So what you mean to say is that you're basically throwing away $24,000 a year?"

"What?"

"You can find a decent apartment for $2,000 a month. You could even find one for less than that if you move to one of the boros and then you would be ahead of the game." says Irina.

"Well, my Dad gives me $1,500 a month every month to let me use as a travel stipend. He says he wants me to be able to travel freely so that money helps a little bit. But right now I'm using most of that money to pay for my car."

"You have a car?" Irina and I said almost at the same time.

"Everyone in LA has a car. I just didn't think garages were going to be so expensive. The cheapest one I found so far is $700 a month plus I heard car insurance is really expensive. Right now I'm still under my mom's insurance so I don't have to pay but pretty soon I will have to cover that myself too."

"Right, but you're not in LA." says Irina

"Why didn't you sell your car before you moved here?" I asked

"I just figured it would be convenient to have a car. How often do you guys rent a car?"

"Almost never." I said.

"I hire a car and driver." Irina says in an exaggerated highbrow tone.

"Yeah, a big advantage to living in the City is that you don't need to own a car." I say.

I noticed that Topaz was suspiciously quiet and listening carefully to the conversation.

"Yeah, I got a big bump in salary, an extra $1,500 then living expenses and they will pay for my rent, well, at least $2,000 towards rent. So I'm sitting pretty. In fact this meal is on me!" she says.

I could tell Topaz could not take it anymore. "Don't you realize the opportunity you have here? You could be saving so much money," she says. "Why don't you take your New York money and save it for when you move back to California?"

"What do you mean? What do I need to save money for?"

"Retirement? Disability? Rainy day."

"Why? I'm still in my twenties."

"But you're blowing like $60,000 a year, probably more. In five years with a relatively conservative indexed investment plan that's over $350,000 just down the drain."

"What? How do you figure?"

At that moment two servers arrived with big trays. They unloaded the smorgasbord of foods in front of us and everything looked great. To my surprise our sangria pitcher was empty and she brought a fresh one. I was starving I thought to myself

Once the food arrived all talk of finance went by the wayside. I can't believe I've never been to this place before and I never really thought about happy hour. To me happy hour always seemed like a place that harried executives went to so they could knock back a few bourbons before going home to the wife and kids or some bar that was loud and obnoxious full of frat boys. I didn't realize it could include gourmet food. I may have to start going to more happy hours rather than full dinners. These small plates were just the right size anyway.

As the girls talked my mind drifted a little bit and begin to wonder what I would have done if I was in Francesca's position. It sounded like she had the world handed to her. And I don't mean to say that I'm jealous but I wasn't making that kind of money when I was her age nor did I have a "travel stipend" from good ol' Dad. I think for sure my retirement account would be considerably larger than it is now. Plus I would probably own my apartment rather than renting. I don't really think that much about finances but I know I want to own my own home. I'm sure that I should have some sort of insurance as well like life insurance or disability or long-term care but that sounded like something I should take care of when I was older anyway.

"What do you think, Mel?"

I snapped back to reality, Topaz was talking to me while Irina and Francesca we're both looking at me expectantly.

"I'm sorry, what?"

"What would you do with a million dollars?" repeats Topaz.

"I don't know." I stammered "I never really thought about it. I guess I would pay off my bills and invest."

"I would just hire Topaz and let her do her thaaaaaang," says Irina.

Topaz laughed. "The Force is strong in this one." she said in a Yoda like voice.

"I'd travel around the world for a year with my friends," says Fran-K. "Or at least until we got bored. I'd probably hang out in Prague for a while and just chill, maybe do something for a charity."

"What would you do, Tim?" I ask.

Topaz poured us all more sangria while she obviously stalled for time to formulate her answer. She then takes a sip of her sangria and started talking.

"I'm not sure why one million dollars is the magical number but people often ask me what I would do if I was given a million dollars to invest for them. My answer is always the same: it depends. What you would do with a certain amount of money at any given time depends on your particular life situation, where your other investments are and what your end goal is with the money. A millennial like Fran-K wants to take the money and go spend it on experiences. Melissa who is established in her career and already has retirement goals in mind may want to just pay off bills and set up her nest egg. While somebody like Irina who is getting married has completely different goals. She may want to use it to pay for her wedding or to make a down payment on a home. It's all going to depend on where you are right now. The best way that I can answer this is to think about the different ways money can be invested."

"Oh god," interrupted Irina, "is this going be more boring financial talk?"

"Drink your sangria! I promise this is simple." replies Topaz as she grabs a cocktail napkin.

Topaz drew a big X and then a little dollar sign, a graph that look like it represented the stock market, a dice and a lock.

"Okay let's pretend each one of these quadrants represents a type of money. The dollar sign represents the cash that you have on hand. It could be in a money market account, in your safe or a savings account. It's just something that you can access easily. In the financial world we call this liquid assets. You're not really earning any money on it but you can get to it whenever you need it. You always need to have money in this quadrant. How much money you need to have on hand is going to depend on your particular lifestyle. As we just witnessed having only $300 for a week was not adequate for Melissa. You want to think about how much money you want to have on hand that has to be available immediately. You don't want this to be a large number because you want your money working for you but you don't want to have a serious situation and have to scramble to get out of investments that are going to cost you money in fees or capital loss."

"So, like $500?" I ask.

"No, I would say general rule of thumb is somewhere between 2-6 month's expenses."

"Oh, that makes sense." I say.

"The next quadrant" Topaz says as she points to the graph "is made of money that is invested into the market. It will go up and down and it's money that you don't need right away. You should expect somewhere between 5%- 9% return on this money on average."

"You mean like stocks?" says Irina.

"Sure. Really any money that is invested in the market, it could be within your 401k, stocks, mutual funds, ETFs, just whatever money that will fluctuate with the market."

"OK, I get that."

Topaz then points to the dice. "This is money that is invested in every place but the market. I hate using dice here as a placemark but it really is high-risk high-reward scenario. It's not gambling but this is money that's typically not liquid and you normally will need to be in the investment between three and five years but the reward can be really high. You do have the possibility of losing it all but it's good to have money in this category because it gives you the opportunity to make better than market gains. Also this is typically a good place to have your money when the market is doing poorly. You could put money into commodities, real estate, precious metals, REITs, oil, private equity, you name it. If you're qualified, this is a wonderful way to diversify your portfolio when you are ready to take on more risk.

"I'd rather go to Vegas!" says Fran-K.

"If you put $250,000 into each category, would you take $250,000 to Vegas?"

"Whoa! No. I might take $25,000 though." Fran-K winks

"Fine. Then just find nine other places to put $25,000 so you can diversify your alternative investments."

"Oh, I get it, so like you're diversifying your risk."

"Absolutely. The alternative world is full of good investments but nothing is a sure thing. Every investment sounds awesome in the beginning, but not all of them are going to be super stars."

"That makes sense." I say.

"Now for last quadrant, the one with the lock on it; this is money that is protected."

"Like by the FDIC?" says Fran-K

"No, the FDIC is for bank products like your checking account or a CD. They cover a certain amount in case of something like a bank failure. I think right now they cover up to $250,000 per person, but you want to confirm with your bank."

"Then what do you mean protected?"

"These are typically products by insurance companies. There are a host of products out there that will allow you to participate in the market and receive gains but your money is protected from loss. "

"Oh, that's cool." says Fran-K.

"It is; especially when used the right way. So basically you've got four categories of money: one would be the liquid money (your cash), one would be money that's in the market (like stocks), one that's completely independent of the market called alternative investments and money that is protected."

Topaz leans back and drinks some more of her sangria. Everyone is a little bit lost in thought probably mentally calculating what they would do with their million dollars.

" I don't get it" says Irina with a confused look on her face.

"Which part?"

"Well of course I understand the cash part. That's just the money you have in the bank or on your person I get that. But you said that there's money that's in the market, money that's protected from the market and then money that's independent of the market."

"Yup."

" I don't understand that."

Topaz grabbed her phone. She punched a few buttons and turned the screen around to Irina.

"Oh god, I saw those! They're gorgeous!"

Topaz then showed the screen to Fran-K and me, on the screen were an elegant pair of turquoise and gold spiked stilettos. They were outrageous but stunning.

"Wow. Those are pretty!" says Fran-K.

Topaz asks, "Would you buy them? They're $1,000 and supposedly will be THE shoe next Spring."

"I don't know. It seems risky. I'm not a big fan of turquoise but if turquoise actually does hit the runway in the Spring those would be the most perfect shoes. I can wear them with almost anything. But if turquoise didn't catch on then I'd be stuck with a dud and I would have wasted a thousand dollars on shoes that I didn't really want. I'd probably end up selling them on eBay for like $400 after wearing them twice."

"Okay but what if you bought them today and they turned out to be the most amazing shoes? Everyone wanted them and they were limited edition. What if the Spring hit and nobody could find the size that you have and you could sell them for $1,800?"

"Hot damn, I'd be up $800! I'd totally sell them."

"Great." Topaz points to the dice quadrant and says that's a little bit what an alternative investment is like. You think that it's a good deal, you do your research and it could really do well but you have just as much of a chance of it not doing well. It wouldn't be a total loss but you would have to be comfortable losing some money."

"Oh, that totally makes sense! Like, don't buy it with your rent money."

"Exactly!"

"What's this one?" she points to the lock.

"Protected money? Think of that as your little black dress. If you buy the right LBD it can be in style for years. It's a safe investment and worth having in your closet. Everybody should have several LBDs to choose from."

"Why didn't you explain it like this in the first place? This makes sense!" says Irina and points to the graph quadrant representing the market.

"Money that participates in the market? Well that would be like having a Louis Vuitton Neverfull or Alma. These bags are classic and never go out of style but they do sometimes go out of favor. So there's going to be times when you have one on your arm and everyone else does too. That's when their value is a little less and there's going to be other times when it's come back en vogue and you could sell yours at a profit.

When you invest in the stock market and you pick strong companies or indexes they are going to go up and down but over the long term the stock market has a good average return. So you think about your investments for the long haul like you would a classic Louis Vuitton handbag."

Irina clapped her hands. "This totally makes sense. So basically what you're saying is that everyone should have money that's invested in the market and have protected money but only put money into alternative investments if you can really afford it."

"Exactly. There's some requirements for most alternative investments that you'll have to go over before putting your money into those types of investments, but even if you are qualified you shouldn't put your money somewhere until you really understand the risks and fees associated."

"This is cool. I never had anybody explain money like this with examples it makes a lot more sense to me now. So before you were saying I was wasting like $60,000 a year?" says Fran-K excitedly.

"That's approximate. You might be spending more than that I wouldn't know without looking at the whole picture. If you were to downsize and get into an apartment that's fits your $2,000 a month allowance then you have an additional $2,000 a month to invest."

"OK. so what do I do with that $24,000? Put it into high risk stuff since I'm young?"

"If that's all the money you have then absolutely not. Do you have a 401k at work? Does your employer do matching? Are you maximizing your free money? Do you have a life insurance policy?"

"Life insurance? No, that's for old people. Why on Earth would I want life insurance when I am still in my twenties?"

"You would want to get life insurance because you're in your twenties and are healthy. If you get a permanent life insurance policy now when you're young it could be paid off by the time that you're in your forties. I don't like to talk about negativity but if something happened like maybe you start getting seizures or some other medical condition, God forbid, you would not be able to get life insurance later on. If you get it now when you're healthy you have at least locked in your premiums. Plus you can use it as a way to participate in the market."

"Life insurance can be an investment?"

"Some types, yes."

"Like in the stock market?"

"Sure. There's all sorts of ways you can invest with life insurance, it just depends on what product you have and what they offer. It's a great place to start and it will be inexpensive right now."

"Can't I invest something more interesting? Life insurance sounds kind of boring to me. Could I put money into the stock market?"

"Trust me if you knew all the things you could do with life insurance you wouldn't think that it was boring but I understand where you're coming from. I used to think life insurance was boring too. But absolutely you can put money into the stock market and you should. If you qualify for a Roth IRA that would be one of the first places I would suggest you put your money and put in the maximum every single year that you qualify."

"I have heard of a Roth but I'm not really sure what it is."

"That's OK. Most people don't know what a Roth is and I'm glad you asked. I think one of the most important things you can do when talking about your finances is ask questions. A lot of people feel silly or dumb when they don't know what something is that is being discussed so they just nod their heads instead of asking because they don't want to appear uninformed. A Roth and a 401K are both IRAs. Do you know what an IRA is?

We all nodded our heads.

"I know it has something to do with retirement," I said.

"Yup! IRA stands for Individual Retirement Account. So both the Roth and the 401K have the same limitations: you can not take your money out until your age 59½."

"What if you get into a bind and you need it anyway?" asks Irina.

"Sure. Life happens. Sometimes you have to pull money from there but that should be the last place that you take money from. On top of taxes that you may need to pay you will have a 10% penalty on the money you withdraw before 59½."

"Ouch" I said.

"Ouch is right. The difference between a 401K and a Roth is that the 401K is invested with pre-tax dollars and you pay the taxes when you're in retirement. The theory being that when you retire you will be in a lower tax bracket than you are today. We don't know if that will actually be true but it allows you to have more money to invest today and then pay taxes later."

"I don't understand that." says Fran-K, "What do you mean pre-tax?"

"It is money that is taken out of your paycheck prior to your employer taking taxes out."

"Oh, Duh. OK. So How do you pay for a Roth account then?"

"Don't feel like that was a silly question. Asking for clarification is always OK. The Roth account is paid for with after-tax dollars so it's the same as if you buy anything else. The cool thing about the Roth is that it will grow tax-free and it will pay out tax free. That's a pretty good deal which is why there's a limit of how much money you can put in each year like right now it's $5,500 annually. The maximum amount changes so you'll want to check with your tax professional."

"So really everybody should have a Roth account."

"Well, not everybody can qualify. But usually it's a good thing to invest in if you have the money and meet the criteria. Just remember you can't touch this money until you're actually 59½."

"Right or pay a 10% penalty." says Fran-K.

The server returned and asked if we wanted dessert. We all opted to have a little more sangria instead of dessert and then take a walk to burn the calories. While the waitress was clearing our plates and getting us another pitcher of sangria it was obvious that Fran-K was lost in thought.

"OK, so I get why I should have moved into some place that was cheaper but if I did have extra money to save every single month what should I be doing besides the Roth and life insurance? You said something about long-term care insurance?"

"Yes, long-term care insurance is important. More people go bankrupt from medical bills than any other reason. A lot of times what you'll see is that as people get older and their health fails, they use up their retirement savings paying the medical bills. What often happens to couples is the majority of their savings is used for one spouse's medical bills and then when that spouse passes the other spouse is left trying to live on what little money that remained, most of which could be prevented if they had a long term care option in place."

"That's terrible!"

"It is but it happens all the time. However, 20 is a little bit too young for long-term care insurance, I mean I'm not against it but it's not as much of a priority when you're in your prime as it is for somebody in their forties and fifties."

"Prime?!" says Irina, "I'm still in my prime even if I'm not 20!"

"I know, hun, but if you wait until you need long term insurance, it may not be affordable, so that's why you think about long term care options in your 40s and 50s. Historically women have lived longer than men and in the financial world we call this longevity risk."

"Longevity risk?" ask Irina.

"Yes, people are living much longer than they had in the past thanks to healthier living and better medical care. People often will outlive their money, women especially and this risk is called a longevity risk."

"Wait! What do you mean outlive your money?"

"Once you retire, you will still have expenses so you have to take into consideration where that retirement income will be coming from. A lot of people don't take health care costs into consideration and they completely forget about inflation. So while your spending habits might be the same when you're 80 as it was when you were 60, the cost of goods may have increased and you may have more health care costs."

"Oh, you mean how like my grandmother says a loaf of bread used to be a nickel and now it's like 5 bucks at Whole Foods?"

"Well, that's a little bit extreme but yes. Think about how much a Louis Vuitton handbag was 20 years ago. And I realize that a Louis Vuitton handbag is not a necessity but it does give you a good idea of what inflation is all about. Rent prices, gas prices, food prices and health care especially all of these things go up considerably every decade. So, as women, we have longevity risk because we live longer and our money won't last if it wasn't invested properly or we did not save enough to begin with. Throw in medical problems that require long-term care and your money disappears even faster."

"What does long-term care actually mean?"

"That is pretty straightforward. Basically there's something called ADL which stands for activities of daily living. There are six basic ADLs: eating, bathing, dressing, toileting, transferring (walking) and continence. If something happens to you where you are unable to perform at least two of the six activities of daily living then you qualify for long-term care. Usually there's a period of time like 90 days before the long-term care insurance will actually kick in but depending on what type of long term option you have in place it can provide money for anything from just medical expenses to actually providing income."

"Oh shit! I think that's what happened to my friend's dad. He was on his way somewhere and got his finger stuck in a car door and he was a surgeon and now he can't operate anymore but they have insurance and that covers like his income or something."

"Well it is possible that that is long-term care but more than likely that's disability insurance."

"Oh," says Fran-K, "what's the difference between disability insurance and long-term care insurance?"

"Well, while both help protect you in case of health issues, disability insurance helps replace your income in the event of a disability. So what you're describing sounds more like disability insurance than long-term care. Long-term care is typically used to pay for Long-Term Care

Health costs not to replace your income, like if you have a stroke or are disabled."

"Oh, I think that makes sense. Should I get disability insurance?"

"Well disability insurance is a pretty good thing to have but it just really kind of depends. It's not that expensive generally around 3 to 5% of your income depending on what you need and what type of riders you get added to it but someone who is active in their work, like for instance your friend's dad who was a surgeon or a hair stylist or a physical therapist if something happens to their hands they would not be able to work in their chosen profession. If that happens then that 3 to 5% of their income to replace 50%-70% of income sounds pretty good, right?"

"No kidding."

"But for you in your twenties as a social media guru, disability insurance probably is not your top priority."

"I'm so stressed out! I didn't realize there was so much to finances."

"Don't be stressed out. I'm just answering some questions for you but I feel like it's good to know your options. What would have happened to your friend's dad if he didn't have insurance to cover his hand injury?"

"I don't know. Her mom is also some type of doctor but I know they said he spent more years in school then he did practicing and they had a huge school loan to pay off. He still works part time I think in a school or does seminars or something like that but the amount of money they were thinking he would bring in is way less than what he makes now."

"Then it sounds like they would have been in a pretty bad situation if he hadn't had the insurance policy in place."

"Oh, for sure that does sound like it made a big difference I never really thought about it until just now."

"That is a common problem. Most people don't think about long-term care or disability insurance until it's too late."

"Topaz, what were you saying about me setting up a trust before I get married?"

"How about we talk about that later? I would like to talk more about the sangria and those turquoise stilettos right about now."

"Cheers to that!" Irina said.

We finished the pitcher of sangria and continue to talk about what we thought the fashion trends were going to be this Spring. We all shared horror stories of poor fashion decisions in the past. I can kind of see why Topaz used fashion to help explain the market. It is a lot easier to understand something when put into terms that you already know. That's the thing that always put me off with most financial people is they used all these terms that I had never heard before. I guess it's the same way with law, when I speak in legalese people have a hard time understanding me unless they're also attorneys. But I don't know why financial people talk to laymen in financial terms because they're the only ones that understand what's being said.

THE FUTURE

The rest of the evening was spent making small talk while walking along the Hudson in hopes of burning off the calories from the sangria and tapas. Francesca seemed sweet albeit a bit naïve about how the world works. She doesn't know how good she has it, but then, I thought, who does know what they're doing in their 20s?

I got home, cleaned my apartment and laid out my clothes for the next day. On a whim I logged into my bank account and checked the balance

After checking the balances of my checking and savings accounts, I wrote them down. Then I logged into my corporate benefits website and looked at my portfolio. It was very confusing because there was profit sharing, deferred stock and my 401k all lumped together. I couldn't tell what exactly I was invested in but it seem like I was doing okay. I wrote down that number too.

Satisfied that I have done my financial part for the day I was happy to be off my $300 a week budget. Although I have to say I was very grateful for the experience because now I will get bagels by the house instead of the office. Topaz had given me back my credit cards so that was a sense of relief. Before this exercise I had not realized how frequently I use my credit card. But it was so much easier than cash. I decided to give myself a $400 budget for the following week. I felt like my budget should really be around $200 a week if you didn't factor in my trainer, dry cleaning or transportation. I also decided that I would cut my trainer down to once a week and give myself a three month limit and reevaluate after 90 days to see if it was worth having a personal trainer. I do OK but I'm not made of money and after listening to Topaz today I definitely wanted to make sure that I was doing as much as I could for my financial future. What had she called it? Longevity risk?] I would hate to run out of money in my old age. I thought briefly about being old, eating cat food and living on welfare.

I woke up the next morning before my alarm clock and got dressed quickly so that I could use the bagel guy down the street rather than the one by the office. I had no idea if there would be a line or not. But I was determined to lower the cost of my morning breakfast. I got ready for work and rode the elevator down with other neighbors in silence. I wished the doorman a good day as I passed him in the lobby and went down my front steps. To my dismay the bagel guy that I had just discovered was gone. But there was another guy across the street with a short line in front of him. I walked over to that bagel cart and it had a special listed for a coffee with bagel and cream cheese for $2.50! Bingo!

As I rode the subway to work I tried to do the math in my head. If I had discovered this bagel guy three years ago when I moved in then let's see, $1.75 savings per day times 20 days per month times 12 months times 3 years... well I don't know what that comes to exactly but it's over $1,200. Imagine if I did something like this with every purchase I made I thought to myself. I always considered budget as the B-word but this wasn't even difficult; it was more like self-awareness. I felt a little sick to my stomach that there are probably multiple purchases I make on a regular basis that with just a tiny bit of effort I could be saving a lot of money over the course of time. I decided to ask Topaz if she would help me figure out my budget. Although maybe that's not something for a financial advisor to do, maybe that's just something I need to do on my own. I vowed to put my expenditures in the ledger for another week. If I did that I would have a better understanding of what I spend money on regularly. Maybe I should do the ledger like the way Irina did it so I could get a true understanding of what I really spend normally. I know for a fact that it's not $1,100 a week but it is probably closer to $500 a week which if you think about it is like $24,000 a year.

I walked into my office determined to live a life where I am more aware of the money I spent so that I am not frivolously blowing my potential financial future. I started thinking about how much money I would need in retirement. Even though retirement was another 20 or 30 years off if

I continue to live in New York City the expenses would just continue to rise. I guess Topaz was right that I shouldn't put this off until I get married. I should plan for my own personal financial future and then when I meet the right guy we can merge our financial plans together. I know I wouldn't want to date somebody who didn't have their money matters in order. I don't suppose it's a big criteria for most guys, I thought to myself but surely that would make me a more attractive mate than one who was unaware of their spending.

The rest of my day flew by and I was very productive for a Monday. I actually left on time for once. On my way to the subway I called Greg. I hadn't talked to him since Friday when I declined his dinner invitation. It was unusual that I didn't hear from him so I had a little trepidation about calling. However he answered on the first ring and sounded happy to hear from me. I asked if he wanted to go for a walk along the river and maybe get a glass of wine at happy hour. He said that sounded like a great idea and we agreed to meet in half an hour.

When I got home I changed into something a little more casual and went back outside to meet at our normal spot. Greg was already waiting there for me.

"Hello beautiful it is great to see you." he kissed me warmly on the mouth.

I didn't realize how much I had missed him until that moment.

"Thank you. How was your day?"

"Better now" he said smiling at me. "I thought something was going on when you declined dinner on Saturday." He took my hand and we began walking down the Promenade.

"No, nothing was wrong I just was not having a very good week."

"Why? What happened? Is everything okay?"

"Everything is fine it is just that Tim had us doing an experiment."

Greg raised his eyebrows and slyly asked me "What kind of experiment? Anything I want to know about? Are there pictures?" he said jokingly.

I elbowed him. "No, not that kind of experiment."

I told him all about the ledger Topaz had given Irina and me and what I had to do for the week. I explained what I learned about the bagels and then I told him about how upset Irina was with her spending. I didn't tell him how much she spent because I didn't think it was right to share her personal information but I did mention how shocked she was at the amount that she spent. Then I told him how upset I had been not having enough money for the week and why I turned down dinner with him.

He stopped briefly and gave me a big hug. "You never have to worry about money when you're with me." he said.

"Why not?" I asked.

"Because I am very careful with my money. I would not ask you out if I could not afford to take you out."

"I never really thought of you as frugal."

"Oh, I wouldn't say frugal, call me a Mindful Spender."

Hmm, I thought, mindful spender, that made a lot of sense. I guess being frugal would be eating breakfast at home, being a mindful spender is finding a cheaper bagel guy. I liked the phrase and decided to adopt it as my own.

"Well, why does paying have to fall on the man?"

"I like doing it." he said "I like taking care of you."

"That's so sweet." I said and squeezed his hand.

"I'm surprised you lasted on $300."

"Really? I thought that amount was actually pretty high."

"It is really high. I know that there are all sorts of experiments where people try to eat on $1 a day or $2 a day when they're really trying to cut their budget down. So $40 a day should be more than enough."

"Then why are you surprised I had a hard time lasting on $300?"

"Because I have watched how you spend money."

I thought about this for a moment and asked "Do you think that's an unattractive quality?"

"Well, it is none of my business how you spend your money. But if we took our relationship to the next level and had joint accounts it is definitely something I would want to address."

"Oh. I never thought about it like that."

"Don't worry! I hate to spoil the surprise but I'm definitely getting you a subscription to People magazine for Christmas."

I blushed a little. "I didn't even know you knew I read that magazine."

"I did get a kick out of it. It does not seem like the type of material you would typically read. But I couldn't believe you were paying newsstand prices when it's like I don't know a quarter of the price if you would just get a subscription. Every now and then they have all sorts of deals where it seems like it's 90% off or something. All I know is that if you buy any kind of magazine on a regular basis you should definitely subscribe to it."

"So I'm finding out…." I said lost in thought. "Do you have a 401K?"

"What? Yes, of course. Why?"

"Topaz was telling us about the ways that you invest money. She talked about four different categories. She said basically there's liquid money, protected money, market money and alternative investments. She said eventually we want to have money in all categories. Do you know what's she talking about?"

Greg laughed. "Yes, of course I do. Guys talk about this kind of stuff all the time. Don't you discuss investments with your girlfriends?"

I looked at him like he had two heads. "No. We really never do talk about money."

"Why not?"

"I don't know. I always thought it was very confusing. But then Topaz explained it and it makes a lot more sense now. Do you have money in all the categories?"

"Yes, I do. I don't have much in alts though."

"Alts?"

"That is what my financial advisor calls it. He shortens alternative investment to alts."

"Oh. good to know the lingo."

"Yes, it takes a while to catch on to what they're saying. Honestly most of time I have no idea what he's talking about. But I am in a REIT."

"What's a REIT?"

"Basically it's real estate. Think of it kind of like a mutual fund except for with real estate. It stands for Real Estate Investment Trust. I don't really understand it. My advisor spent a lot of time explaining it to me and it made sense to me at the time. What I do know is that I get monthly dividends on it that gets automatically reinvested back into the REIT.. I can't get to the money for a couple of years but that's okay. The returns I'm getting are pretty good. I didn't want to put too much money in there because it does sound a little bit risky to me especially after the big housing crash that we had a couple of years ago. But I did want to be able to have an opportunity to earn better than what my stock portfolio is doing. So I took a baby step and bought a REIT that he said was pretty conservative."

"Topaz said that alts were a way to diversify?"

"That is exactly what my financial advisor said too. He said since I rent and don't own a house that this is a way for me to be investing in real estate with a whole lot less money. I didn't put much money in and I would be okay if I lost all of it. He said that it would be very unlikely for me to lose all of it but it could happen. He also explained that this is illiquid investment and that it could do poorly and it could take years for me to get my money back."

"That's kind of scary."

"Well, most investments don't have any guarantees anyway, so I was comfortable with this REIT. I've had it for almost two years and have gotten 10% returns each year. If it keeps going like this in another year or two I will get my original investment back plus those dividends. I'm pretty happy."

I couldn't believe that Greg had all this already set up. We were the same age and I hadn't given any of this any thought yet. I suddenly blurted out "Do you have life insurance, long-term care insurance or disability insurance?"

Greg stopped. "Is there something you need to tell me? Do you have a skydiving trip planned for us?" he laughed.

I realize how silly my questions were out of context. "No, it was just this is the first time that any of this had ever been explained to me. I feel like I need to go out and get disability insurance right away."

"Well, don't feel bad. My father started teaching me about this when I was little. In fact when I was born he bought me my own life insurance policy."

I felt a little bit behind the curve. I wondered why my parents had never talked to me about money.

Greg and I talked a little bit more about his portfolio. I wasn't curious about how much money he had in it but more his reasons behind each purchase. After what Topaz had said yesterday and how she explained the different types of investments it was all making a lot more sense to me.

After happy hour Greg walked me back to my building. I did realize that knowing how financially savvy my boyfriend was made him slightly more attractive. I felt a little guilty for that thought but then I realized it wasn't about the money, it's just felt nice to know he was preparing for the future. I vowed to do the same thing.

● ○ ● ○ ● ○ ●

The rest of the week flew by. I passed Francesca a few times in the lobby but didn't see Irina or Topaz. I continued to put my purchases in the ledger. I didn't buy any magazines that week, nor did I dine out. I was now on a mission to save more money. I wondered how people lived on $1 a day, obviously that wasn't in NYC and it was probably an old study.

By the time Friday rolled around I had become a reformed consumer. Whenever I spent money I was mindful about each purchase. I'm not sure how much money I saved but I definitely had made a life-changing mindset about what I would buy and where. I hadn't actually added up all my expenditures for the week but my mental tally was around $200. Making some minor changes made a big difference.

I left work relatively early on Friday and as I was walking out of the train station I spotted Topaz on the sidewalk walking towards our building.

"Hey stranger." I said

"Meeeeeeeeeel!" she said when she turned around and gave me double air kisses.

Topaz looked fabulous as usual. She was wearing a really nice scarf I couldn't tell what it was but I don't think this one was Hermes. But it was just as vibrant and gorgeous. I noticed that since she returned from Paris she was dressing a lot more classic than you typically would see in New York. It was a good look for her.

"You look amazing" I said

"Thank you, darling. Don't you love my scarf?"

"I was just looking at it is Hermes?"

"No, it's classic Christian Lacroix. I found it in a vintage shop in Paris."

"I like it."

"Thank you."

"Do you have time this weekend to talk about my finances?"

"Mais, Oui! I'd love to help you however I can. How about right now?"

"Now? Well OK."

"No better time than the present. Is there anything specific that is bothering you?"

"Nothing specific but just in general I have a lot of questions. I was thinking about what you said about how women don't really focus on finances. Then I talked to Greg yesterday about what you would said and what I've learned with the budget and he already has money and all the categories that you talked about."

"That's fantastic. I love financially savvy men. You have a good one there!" she says.

"I have to admit learning that he'd already thought about his future and made plans did make him even more attractive to me. We didn't talk about amounts but just his plans. He said his father even bought him life insurance when he was a baby."

"That's really good. That used to be a pretty common practice back in the day. I don't see it as frequently now but it's still a great thing to set up for your child. As they get older they can use the cash value to like make loans to themselves like for college or a down payment on a house. It's a great investment. I'd be real interested in seeing his father's portfolio. I've worked with a lot of baby boomers that have very sound financial plans just because their parents went through the Great Depression and had solid fundamentals already in place and passed on these values to their children."

"I bet that would be real interesting."

We walked up the stairs to our building together. The doorman had a package for Topaz and I told her that I would drop my things off at my place and come up to her apartment shortly. I walked down the hallway to the elevator wondering if my parents were set up financially. Maybe I should have Topaz talk to them as well. I wondered how my father would respond to receiving advice from someone younger than him. But then people talk to doctors younger than them all the time. It's really about expertise and not age. I can't recall him ever actually talking about a financial advisor. I know he talks about his CPA maybe that's the person who does his financial planning I thought. I got on the empty elevator and hit 12 for my floor. I was lost in thought about not just my finances but about my parents' as well. Both of my parents were in really good health. I really don't have any idea how much money they made but my mom has only ever worked part-time. I wondered if longevity risk was an issue that they had addressed. I made a mental note to talk to them about this at Sunday dinner.

I changed clothes and looked for the note that I had scribbled my balances on. I grabbed my ledger and was about to walk out the door when I remembered the wine I had bought earlier in the week. It was

French and red and it was on sale two for $18. It said Côtes du Rhône Villages on it I didn't know if that was good or not but at least I wasn't showing up empty-handed.

I walked down the hall to the elevator bank and hit the up arrow button. Topaz lived on the top floor. Her apartment was almost identical to mine structurally but from an energy perspective our two apartments couldn't be any more different. Her walls were painted gold and had little flecks of glitter everywhere. She had trinkets and items from all over the world scattered throughout her apartment it definitely gave it a vibrant vibe about it and I really enjoyed being there. It was quite blissful to me as her place always smells great and she had wonderful music playing in the background. My apartment on the other hand was the kind of apartment you'd expect a corporate attorney to have. It was sparse and neutral save a bright red lamp shade I bought on a whim about six months ago. Oddly enough just making that one change dramatically improved my mood. It is interesting to me how one small change can have such a huge impact. I guess that's like me switching where I buy my bagels. One little move can save me for $500 a year. Just like a small investment in a red lamp shade changed my mood every single time I walked into my apartment. It really is important to appreciate the little things in life.

The elevator bell announced its arrival on my floor. The door opened to an empty car and I pressed 36. The elevator quickly zoomed over to 36 and when the doors opened I walked out towards Topaz's apartment; she was only a couple of doors down from the elevator which was nice, my apartment was all the way at the end of the hall. I had barely knocked on the door when it opened. In fact my hand was still midflight into the second knock. Topaz saw the surprise registered on my face.

"I heard the bell ring, I figured it was you."

"Oh! Hah. That's nice. I brought wine." I held up the bottle for her inspection.

"Côtes du Rhône Village!" she said sounding very French. "Great value!"

"Thanks. It was on sale. I did a lot better this week with my budget and decided to splurge."

"Do you mind if I ask how much you paid?"

"How much should I have paid?" I asked curiously.

"Well, this wine is a blend and you never really know what you're going to get. The wines that say Village are sometimes slightly better than the ones that don't. In France this is a very inexpensive wine, some places use it as a table wine. I would guess $11 or $12 a bottle?

Pleased with my purchase I said "They were 2 for $18!."

"Bravo. That's great. Let's try it and if we like it maybe we should go buy a couple more bottles. I love wines that are great and inexpensive. Now that the California wines are more in favor than the French ones, you can often find stores dropping the prices on great French wines so they can move inventory."

"I never really thought about wine trends."

"Well, it's like anything. The things that are popular or convenient are going to have the higher prices. It's just general supply and demand. If you think about things that are not in high demand, usually those things will be lower in price. For instance the point of sale items that are near the cash register? Without exception there is almost always a cheaper brand somewhere else in the store but this is in a premium space and they're counting on impulse buys. Like when you go to the grocery store the most expensive items are eye level because they're the easiest ones to see. Or like when Uber is more expensive when the bars let out because everyone needs a ride and there's not enough drivers. If you think about purchases in every format from a supply and demand situation you can almost always save money. Think about all the people that go out of town by car on a three-day weekend. Gas stations hike up the prices on those weekends. So when you know a three-day weekend is coming up try to fill up by Wednesday morning rather than waiting until Friday evening."

"That makes sense. I never thought about it like that. Not that I have a car."

"You will start thinking in that way. Sometimes supply and demand works out in your favor. If a store purchases a lot of an item expecting a huge influx of purchases but then doesn't received the business, then you might get an item that should be in high demand but has very low prices. The more you become aware of what you're spending your money on and how much you're paying the more you will be able to save money."

"Right. Like the bagel guy."

Topaz laughs. "You and your bagels!"

"Well, I'm saving $1.75 a day! With all of the changes I have been making I am probably saving $100 per week. That's $400 a month! Or...." I did some quick math, "$4,800 a year!"

"$5,200 a year."

"What?" I said quickly redoing the math in my head. "$400 a month times 12 months is $4,800 a year."

"Yes, but you are saving weekly. There are 52 weeks in a year. So $100 a week times 52 weeks is $5,200."

"Oh."

"Don't worry. That is a common budget mistake. People think about their monthly expenses and then just multiply them by 12. They think if they need $30 a week for the subway they will just factor in $120 per month or $1,440 per year. But when a month has five weeks in it they're screwed."

"I never thought about that."

"Well, on the positive side if you get paid every other week it's like getting two extra paychecks that you weren't expecting. Most people get paid every two weeks instead of twice a month. So if you got paid $500 a week the majority of people would say they make $2,000 per month. They'd calculate $2,000 per month times 12 months equals $24,000 a year but in reality they're making $26,000 a year!"

"Oh. Good point. I never really thought about that."

"No problem. Secrets of the trade." she laughs and winks at me jokingly as she walks into the kitchen.

I follow her into the kitchen which had a delightful aroma to it. I wonder what she cooked that smelled so good. Topaz got out a corkscrew and expertly uncorked the wine. She dramatically held the cork under my nose for me to smell. I cautiously smell the cork wondering what it's supposed to smell like.

Topaz pulls the cork away from my nose "You goofball it's a plastic cork. It's not going to smell like anything."

"Oh." I said sheepishly while Topaz giggled.

Topaz pours a little bit of wine into a big glass and swirled it around. She sticks her nose all the way into the glass and takes a big whiff. I watched her eyebrows raise up but I wasn't sure if that was a good sign or a bad one. Topaz takes a sip. With her eyes closed she just stands there for a minute as if she's meditating.

"Is it bad?"

"What? No, it's fantastic. I was just thinking about the last time I had a Côtes du Rhône and where I was. Great choice, Melissa! You did a really good job."

She poured me a full glass and then poured some more into her own glass.

"To making good financial decisions!" she raises her glass in a toast.

"To being a Mindful Spender!" I said stealing Greg's phrase.

Topaz grins, "A Mindful Spender? I like that."

"Me too. I stole it from Greg."

We clink glasses and I tried the wine. I thought it was really good. Like it wasn't too fruity or bitter or anything; it was just simple and fun to drink.

Topaz pulled out two small serving bowls. She opened the refrigerator and removed a jar of olives and some cubed cheese. She put the olives into one bowl and the cheese into the other. In another cabinet she procured a little serving tray, two small plates, two cocktail napkins and a tin of toothpicks. She motioned for me to follow her into the other room. I grabbed the bottle of wine and sat down at her little table. Topaz was arranging our snacks on the tabletop. She had a vase with flowers arranged delightfully that smelled very nice. She moved it over to make room for the bottle of wine.

"So what is on your mind?"

"Well, really everything. Until our brunch with Irina I never really thought about money. I just seemed to have put my financial planning on hold because I'm not married yet. And I know that sounds silly but for some reason that's what I've been doing. I felt like that phase of my life didn't begin until I had a spouse. Now that I think about that that seems ridiculous. In fact when I was talking to Greg about what you were saying I asked him if he had money in all four categories. He said he did and even had alts." I used the shortened word for alternative investment so I could be speaking Topaz's language. She just nodded.

"Really? What type of alts is he in?"

"He says he just has a small amount of money in a REIT."

"That's a great place to start."

"I hate to admit it, even though we did not talk about dollar figures just the fact that he has all this in place already makes me think of him differently. Like a more suitable mate. And if I think that way surely men think that way as well. Don't you agree?

"I don't know how men think. But something I hope to change with the women I know is to get them to talk more freely about money. And I don't mean bragging I mean talking about investments with your financial peers. When men get into a good investment, they will talk to their peers and like pound their chest saying how they discovered this great investment. Not necessarily talking about amounts but showing off how clever they were to buy into this investment. Women almost never talk that way."

"I know. I realized I received almost no financial advice for my parents whereas Greg's father has talked to him about a lot of things from a very young age."

"That is not uncommon. I think that mindset is changing more and more though. Or at least I'd like to hope so. What specifically is bothering you about your financial plan?"

"Well, the fact that I don't have one." I handed her the piece of paper with my balances on it."

Topaz examined it.

"Why do you have so much money in savings? Is this money for something specific?"

"No. I just didn't know where else to put it and I know it's good to save. Do you think I need to get life insurance?"

"Do you have life insurance?"

"I think so. I'm pretty sure my employer offers me life insurance."

"OK. That's good do you know how much it is?"

"Not really. I think it's like two times my salary?"

"Is it really inexpensive like less than $10 a month?"

"Yeah, that sounds about right."

"Then most likely it is group term insurance. I generally don't count that when I ask somebody how much insurance they have."

"What? Why not?"

"Well, every place has a different type of plan but typically employers offer inexpensive group term insurance but it's only good for a while you're working there. Most of the time once you leave that company the insurance goes away."

"Oh. What do you mean when you say term insurance? What does that mean?"

"Term means it is just for a term of time. Generally it will be 10 , 15 or 20 years."

"What happens at the end of the term?"

"It goes away."

"What? That doesn't make any sense why would you have use term insurance at all then. So I'm just paying for nothing?"

"Term insurance is useful. It is considerably cheaper than permanent insurance because it's just a contract and if nothing happens during the term of time, it's not used. Like car insurance."

"Why is it so inexpensive?"

"Well one of the reasons is that insurance companies almost never pay out on term insurance. Like maybe only 3 or 4% of the time."

"What? Why not? Do people not qualify?"

Topaz laughs. " Well in a manner of speaking, no, they don't qualify."

"That's nuts how can that be? How do insurance companies get away with not paying out term insurance?"

"Because people don't necessarily die within the term of time."

"You have to be dead to be able to collect?"

"Yes, we sometimes joke that we call it 'hope to die' insurance."

"That's pretty morbid."

"It's called life insurance for a reason. If you're still alive they are not going to pay out. There are exceptions like if you're terminally ill and expect to be gone within a short period of time they might pay out some money ahead of time. That's called accelerated death benefit but usually that's found with permanent insurance."

"I am really confused. Why would anybody get term insurance?"

"There are a couple of reasons. Sometimes you will get term insurance for a debt. Let's say that you are married or you have kids and have a 20 year mortgage. You M]might get a 20 year Term Policy to cover the length of that loan so that in the event of your passing within that 20 year period of time the mortgage is paid off in full so that your family can have a house to live in that's paid for completely."

"Oh. That makes sense."

"Another reason would be let's say that you were in your thirties right now and are in great health. But financially you cannot afford a permanent policy. You could get a Term Policy now while you're healthy, and if, God forbid, say 10 years from now you are not healthy you could just convert your Term Policy to a permanent one. Most insurance companies would not require you to take underwriting again. So basically you have locked in your good health."

"Oh, then why wouldn't everybody do that?"

"Because you're just locking in your good health. If you were to get a permanent policy when you're in your thirties you are locking in your age."

"I don't understand."

"Think about it like this: The likelihood of you dying in your twenties is considerably lower than you dying when you're in your sixties, right?"

"Sure. All things considered you are much likelier to live until you're in your sixties because that's when health complications come into play."

"Exactly. So the premiums that you would pay when you're in your twenties would be a lot less than when you are in your sixties. For example let's say a policy is $50 a month for a 20 year old the same policy for a 60 year old could be $600 a month."

"Oh. That makes sense. So what you're saying is if I am healthy and can afford it I should get a permanent policy."

"Yes or a combination of a permanent policy and a term policy. What you need to do is figure out how much total insurance you need."

"How do you figure out how much money you need for your total insurance?"

"That will just depend on what you want to leave behind. If someone is relying on your income, you may want to be able to replace that income. Or if you have a specific amount of money that you would need to leave to your beneficiary you would put that money into it. It just depends. For someone who was married with children most the time they elect to pay off the mortgage, pay for their children's college expenses, any other outstanding debt, pay funeral costs and replace their income. "

I thought about that for a bit.

"That's fair. But what about me? I'm not married, I don't have any siblings or any children. If I died and my parents were still alive I guess I would leave some money to them. But other than that I can't think of anything else I need to cover because I don't have any debt. So why would I even want life insurance?"

"That all depends on who picks up your burial costs. If your parents are on a fixed income and burying you would put them in financial dire straits then you might want a small policy to cover those expenses. If your parents are really well off then that might not be a consideration. However, remember how I said life insurance could be pretty interesting?"

"Yes. Which is why I think you're a little off. There doesn't seem to be anything interesting about life insurance."

"Well it is nice because you can use life insurance for investments. Some life insurance policies will even allow you to have a long-term care rider on it."

"Oh, I wanted long-term care. What do you mean a rider?"

"There are tons of different products out there that will allow you to do a lot of different things. Some of them will allow you to use part of your death benefit to pay for long-term care costs in the event that you need it later on down the road. Some people feel that this is a more effective way to pay for a long-term care policies. In the past long-term care policies have been inexpensive but now with rising healthcare costs they are not as affordable as they have been in the past. So for the people that are reluctant to get long-term care because it may be cost-prohibitive this is a great alternative for them if they qualify. But every carrier is different and all the policies have different nuances and fees associated with it so it's important to talk to your insurance person about this very clearly. I would suggest looking at several different carriers and comparing the benefits and costs associated with that before making a decision."

"So what you're saying is if I actually needed long-term care I might be able to use my life insurance to pay for it but if I didn't need long term care that death benefit could go to whoever my beneficiary is on my policy."

"Yes."

"And what did you mean about it being an investment?"

"Well, with term insurance the amount you pay every month is just the premium. That is the actual cost of insurance. To make the math simple let's say that you were going to buy a $250,000 20 year term insurance policy and the premium is $20 a month."

"OK. $20 a month for 20 years."

"Yes. So if you die within those 20 years, it will pay out $250,000."

"Got it."

"If you don't die during that term of time, the insurance company keeps all of your premiums and you get nothing in return. At the end of the 20 years they rip up the contract and you go your separate ways."

"Right, but I am still alive!"

Topaz laughs. "Yes, you're still alive. But let's say instead that you were going to buy a permanent policy for $250,000 but now they want you to pay $100 a month."

"Whoa! That's a big difference!"

"Remember I'm just using these numbers to make the math easier. But, yes, the price difference will be considerably higher because this a policy you will have for the rest of your life, not just 20 years and they know eventually they'll be paying out that $250,000 to your beneficiary."

"OK. That makes sense"

"So in this scenario let's just pretend that the cost of insurance is still only $20 but now the insurance company wants you to pay $100. You can take that additional $80 and put it into an investment within your policy."

"I am confused."

"There are some types of policies that will allow you to invest that extra money and that money you can put into whatever type of investments that particular life insurance product offers. Those are called cash value life insurance policies. Like for instance you might be able to invest into the S&P 500 Index. Think of it kind of like a small investment account. What will happen over a period of time usually around this 7-15 year mark is that you'll start accruing a decent amount of money in the account. What some people do is they borrow money from their life insurance policy to pay for some big event like their daughter's wedding or a down payment on a home. Some people put a lot of money into their life insurance and then when they're in their 60s will use the cash value to supplement their retirement income."

"I'm confused. You borrow your own money from your life insurance policy? Isn't that just your money?"

"Yes. It's like you're making a loan to yourself. You don't necessarily have to pay it back. If you have an outstanding loan on your policy when you die that money is deducted from your death benefit."

"Oh, so what you're saying is if I took out $50,000 from my $250,000 policy to pay for something and never paid the loan back, when I died my death benefit would only be $200,000?"

"Basically. There might be some interest that you would have to pay but essentially that's how it works. Every carrier is a little different so you'd want to find out what's available on your policy but you have the concept down."

"I can totally see the advantage to that. So what you're saying is I could buy a life insurance policy that I could use to invest in the market, use as life insurance and it could cover long-term care costs all in one product?"

"If you qualify, yes. Remember I am just giving you a basic understanding of what is possible. It's going to depend on the type of product you use and your health. The numbers will be dramatically different but for discussion purposes, yes, you can use your life insurance policy to do a lot more than just pay out your death benefit."

"That's pretty cool."

"See? I told you life insurance is awesome. It has a lot more flexibility than most people realize. Of course , rules change, policies change, your health is a huge factor and your family's medical history can be a factor but there are a lot of possibilities with life insurance that you wouldn't get elsewhere. "

"Awesome. I will have to look into that."

"Yes, and when you do make sure you talk to someone who can show you several different carriers. The insurance companies are all very competitive and have new offerings coming out regularly."

"Thanks, I appreciate this information. What do you think about my 401k?"

"Well, all you have given me is your balance. I can't tell you anything from that." Topaz chuckles.

Disappointed, I said, "Oh. Well, what do you need to know?"

"Find out a couple of things for me. Ask your human resource director if there is employer matching. If there is, ask how much and if you have to be vested."

"Hold on. Let me write that down because it doesn't make any sense to me."

Topaz handed me a pen and paper and repeated what she just said. I looked at what I scribbled down and read it to myself. I really wasn't sure what I was going to be asking. I looked up at Topaz with a confused face. She grinned, patted me on the arm and poured more wine.

"Let me explain what I just said. Most employers will offer some type of matching to employees. It is a nice benefit for employees and often a huge incentive for someone to stay at a company."

"OK. I think that we do matching but I don't really know what that means."

"All companies are going to be different and every plan will be slightly customized but in general let's say your company will match 6%. What that means is you invest up to 6% of your gross salary into your 401k they will match it."

"Match it? Like they're giving me free money?"

"Exactly! Which is why you want to take advantage of employer matching. So if you make $100,000 a year, you could put in $6,000 a year and your employer would also put in $6,000 a year."

"Wow. I hope I'm taking advantage of that."

"If you are not, don't feel bad. I have had so many clients kick themselves because they had been working at a company for a long time and never took advantage of matching. It's important to find out what is available to you. Some companies will match dollar-for-dollar up to a certain percentage and then and then will further match $0.50 on the dollar for every dollar you put in."

"You mean like on top of the $6,000 if I put another $6,000 and they put in another $3,000?"

"Yup."

"That's $9,000 that I wouldn't have had!"

"Pretty good, huh?"

"Yes, it is. What did you mean by vested?" I said, excited that I am getting this financial advice. I sipped my wine and stabbed at an olive. I can't believe how reluctant I was to discuss money, this isn't painful at all, I thought.

"Well, some companies will make you wait a period of time before they will do matching. They might wait until you work there 90 days or even up to a year before they will do matching. Another scenario would be that they would match right away but if you left after one year they would take their matching dollars back or a portion of their dollars back. So that's what I mean by vesting it's important to understand what happens when you leave a firm. Some firms will only vest at the end of the year so if you left a firm in the middle of the year you would lose everything for that year."

"Well, that makes sense. They don't want me to take their money and run."

"No. They don't. Employers offer benefits to entice people to join the firm and keep them. It's expensive to hire someone new because of the learning curve and they want you to stay. But when you do leave some of those benefits disappear. Like group term insurance is a good example. Where some places won't pay out vacation days if you weren't employed there long enough. All of these things are something to consider before changing jobs."

"It's interesting that you brought up vacation days" I said grabbing a piece of cheese.

Topaz topped off our wine glasses and stabbed at an olive.

"Why is that?"

"Because HR just called me the other day and asked me if I wanted to roll over my vacation days or take them as payment. I didn't know they had any cash value."

"That's pretty nice. What are you going to do? I know I would be taking those vacation days."

"Yes, I think that that's what I'm going to do. Thank you so much for explaining this to me. I don't know why I thought that this would be a uncomfortable conversation."

"I told you I am happy to do it. It's always good to go over your finances with an actual financial professional and not just another colleague; just to make sure that you're on the right track. If you have a financial advisor take the opportunity to review your financial plan every couple years with another financial advisor just to make sure that you've covered all your objectives. A lot of times advisors only specialize in one or two areas and there may be an entire portion of your portfolio that is being neglected."

"I don't have a financial advisor."

"You do now" Topaz grinned at me.

"To my new financial advisor." I raised my glass in a toast.

"To having a Financial Plan!" said Topaz toasting me.

"Oh, you said there something else you wanted to know about my 401k?"

"Yes. When you get a chance get me a statement of your 401k."

"Why? You have the balance."

"Because I want to see how it's allocated."

"What do you mean?"

"Most 401K plans have limited amount of choices for you to pick. By default you will often be put into a Target Fund with most plans. What that means is they look at your age and they put you in an age appropriate fund based on the year you would likely retire."

"Huh? I have no idea what you're saying."

"OK. Let's keep the math simple. Let's says in the year 2000 someone is 40 years old. The company anticipates you retiring at 65, so that's 25 years from then. They would put you in the fund for year 2025."

"Oh, that makes sense. What's wrong with that?"

"Absolutely nothing, that's fine for when you're just getting started. But as your 401k grows and you get closer to retirement you have very little diversification. If all of your money is in one fund and that fund does poorly what have you done?"

"I put all my eggs in one basket?"

"That's my girl. So you might want to see if there are some other funds that are performing better than your target fund. You could play around with it and put a third of the money in the target fund, a third in international stocks and a third in large cap stocks for example."

"Oh. So what you're saying is there's probably nothing wrong with where I'm invested now but I could maybe have some other options available to me that could be doing better."

"You never know. You could already be in the best funds that there is but it doesn't hurt to take a look."

TRUST ME

I left Topaz's apartment and walked down the hall to the elevator hitting the down button when I arrived. It was really surprising to me that I had never really discussed any of these financial matters with my parents. I felt like my father was a pretty financially savvy man and my mother is very smart but I don't ever remember her talking about money. I know if I ever end up having kids I will make sure whether they are male or female to discuss financial matters with them. It seems like a very important thing to have a basic fundamental understanding of money at a young age. If you have that basic knowledge, like life insurance or retirement accounts maybe people like Francesca who have great opportunities would be able to utilize them a little better. I know I want every advantage I can for my own kids. My fictional kids that I don't have yet I think to myself laughing.

The elevator arrives and I punch my floor number and as it goes down I start making a mental list of the things I need to do tomorrow at work. I arrive at my floor and walk towards my apartment. When I get to my apartment I see something sticking out from under my floor mat. I've bent down to pick up an envelope with my name on it. I open the envelope as I walk through my apartment door. Recognizing the familiar handwriting I realize that it's from Greg.

Inside the envelope was just a simple index card that read:

> Proud of you. Thought you might like this.

And then there was a series of letters and number that just looked like gibberish. He signed it with just XOXO. I quickly turned the card over but it was blank on that side. I grabbed my phone and called Greg. He answered on the first ring.

"Hey you" he says. "I must have just missed you. I just got home from your place. Did you get my surprise?"

"Yes. I'm so sad I missed you. I was just upstairs at Tim's apartment and we were talking about all this money stuff. I wish I'd known you were stopping by I would have loved to see you."

"Oh that's OK. I just wanted to drop off my surprise. I talked your doorman into letting me up; hope you don't mind."

"Yes. I saw the envelope. But I don't understand. What is it?"

"I was really proud to hear that you are discussing financial matters. I know that for a lot of females that is not something they are very comfortable with. I don't really understand that but I know it's a struggle for a lot of women. So I'm proud that you're making an effort to be more conscientious about what you spend your money on."

I was touched that he was so concerned about my financial future. I am surprised he even gave it a minute's thought.

"It has certainly been a learning experience. Topaz has been talking about 401K plans, insurance policies and all other types of investments that I've heard of but up until now I didn't really know too much about. It's a bit overwhelming I have to admit."

"I have to say I'm really surprised that this is the first time you're learning about these things. These are things that I've been talking about with my friends for years. And, of course, whenever I hang out with my father we discuss investments. But, come to think of it, I don't really know any women who discuss their retirement plans or their investments. I think it's great what you are doing with your friends."

"Me too. I'm excited about my newfound knowledge. I still don't really know what I'm doing but I am determined to make changes in my life so that I will have a more secure and stable financial future. If I don't have to worry about money I know I will sleep better at night at the very least. But, Greg, you're killing me. What is this surprise you dropped off?"

Greg is laughing on the other end of the phone. He knows I am very impatient and I am sure he's loving the mystery.

"I'm serious! What are all these letters and numbers for? It was very sweet of you to bring something by but I really need to know what it is before I explode or something." I say laughing.

"I bought you a yearly subscription to Quicken." He sounded very proud of himself.

I had heard of Quicken but I wasn't really sure what it was and wasn't really sure how to respond. But remembering my manners I said, "That is so thoughtful of you. Thank you so much. But I have no idea what Quicken does."

"It is just one of the many accounting software packages that is out there that you can categorize your investments and expenses using their application rather than writing things down in the ledger that Topaz gave you."

"Oh, that was really thoughtful of you. I don't understand though what the advantage of using software over the ledger that I can carry with me everywhere is though."

"It does more than just allow you to enter information in. It should be able to connect with your bank account and probably your 401K as well. So every time you login you can get a real-time update of where your money is. Plus it's easy to make charts and graphs and compare expenses from one month to another."

Greg was clearly excited about this software and I appreciate how much he was supporting me. I tried to sound excited. And knew that I would try to use it just so he felt like he did a good thing. But this was totally not up my alley. It's one thing to think about finances is completely another to connect everything to the internet and try to make sense of it all.

"Oh, wow. It sounds like it does a lot. Thank you again that was really considerate."

"You're welcome, beautiful. I wanted you to have something to make your finances even easier. But listen, I have to go. I want to hit the gym in the morning before work and I have a meeting at 7 so I'm trying to get to sleep early tonight."

"That's great, Greg, thanks again. Sleep well and I will talk to you tomorrow."

"Sweet dreams."

I ended the call and looked again at the index card he gave me. There was no way I was interested in trying to tackle this tonight. I put the card on my desk for safe keeping.

When I got into bed I was exhausted. I think I was asleep before my head hit the pillow. The next thing I knew it was daylight in my bedroom and birds were chirping. I glanced at the clock just as my alarm went off.

I went through my new routine of getting my breakfast near the house instead of at the office and arrived early. On my way to my desk I ran into Jill. Jill had been in a estate attorney for quite some time and I said hello to her. We exchanged pleasantries as we were walking in the same direction. I thought she would be a great person to ask about trusts.

"Hey, so a friend of mine is about to get married and her financial advisor suggested she get a trust."

"Sounds like a smart financial advisor. I would agree. Is she particularly well off?"

"I'm not exactly sure what her situation is but I know she makes a good living. I think that he makes pretty good money though through his business."

"Does he make good money or is it his family that makes good money?"

"I have no idea. Why? What difference does it make?"

"If it is family money they are going to be very protective of some woman coming in and trying to take away what they work so hard for. Chances are they already have a trust set up. At least if they're smart they do. Divorces can be brutal and can take away a family fortune that they've worked generations to obtain. I would be very protective of my legacy, wouldn't you?"

"I never really thought about it like that but absolutely. So you think she should get a trust before she gets married?"

"I can't answer that question without knowing more about the entire situation but it's not a bad idea."

I rolled my eyes. That was the kind of answer I would give without having all the information as well. I guess that's just kind of how lawyers think these days.

"OK. Let me ask you this: Is there ever a way to know if someone needs a trust. Like absolutely beyond a shadow of a doubt should have a trust?"

Jill thought about this question for a second and adamantly said "If you have a mortgage or you have children you should have a trust."

"Really? It's that cut and dry?"

"I like trusts. This is what I do. So, for me, yes. Would another attorney agree with me? Maybe, maybe not? But the reality of it is that you want to have some legal document in place so if something were to happen to you that your loved ones and family are taken care of and things don't get caught up in the court system or contesting a will or probate or any other areas that are gray. If a trust is set up correctly it lays everything out in the event of every situation so that there are no questions about what your wishes are for your children and how money should be spent."

"Do you think I need a trust?"

"Sweetheart, I'm late for a meeting. If you think you need to trust let's set up a lunch and we can chat about it. But you know I can't answer that question without knowing more information. What's going on? Is there some life event that's happening right now that you haven't told me about?"

"No. Sorry to keep you from your meeting. I've just been thinking a lot about retirement and my finances."

"Better you than me. I hate thinking about money. I need to go see a financial advisor but don't really feel like being yelled at. I'm sure there's a whole bunch of stuff I'm doing wrong."

With that statement Jill hurried off in the direction of a conference room. Which left me thinking how often we put off doing things we don't want to do because we don't want to be yelled at. Like going to the dentist when we haven't been brushing regularly or going to the doctor right after binging over the holiday season.

I made a mental note to tell Jill about Topaz. Talking to her made it easy to discuss my finances because I didn't think I was being scolded. It was more like learning from a nice teacher. Well, a nice teacher in stilettos and sparkly like glitter I thought to myself laughing.

I got to my desk and quickly scanned my inbox. My voicemail indicator was blinking and I didn't feel like checking it yet. I opened up my agenda for the day and saw "Call HR" as the number one item. Wasting no time I dialed up HR and ask to speak to someone about benefits."

After getting switched around to the right person. I learned that my company matches dollar per dollar at 6% up to $3,000 and then after that they match $0.50 on the dollar up to an additional $3,000. So basically $6,000 of free money for the year.

As it turns out although I thought I was maximizing my contribution I had only invested $2,000 last year into my 401K. I asked them to make the change and they said it would show up on the following paycheck.

Pleased with myself I checked off my first item on my agenda and got to work.

● ○ ● ○ ● ○ ●

The rest of the day flew by. Before I knew it it was 6 pm and I was one of the last people left in the office. I realize eating at my desk is not one of the healthiest things but I do get a lot more work done. Which technically means I should be leaving earlier not later I thought to myself.

My commute home was fast as most of the rush hour people had gone home earlier. The trains were on time and I got to my stop in no time. When I emerged from the Metro station I was feeling great and refreshed.

As I was walking towards the stairs to the building I ran into Irina coming from across the street. She saw me first and I would have not have noticed her except for the volume of her voice calling my name from across the street.

We greeted each other and gave one another compliments as usual. I don't know if she was sincere about her comments on my outfit but I know I was. I have no idea how she always looks so amazing. I felt pretty tired and haggard from the long day. However, Irina claimed that I looked amazing. I'll take what I can get when it comes to compliments I thought.

"How is week two of the B-word?" I asked Irina.

"Oh, it's going great. I actually did what you did and just took out money instead of trying to use my credit cards all week. It's really hard." moans Irina.

"Tell me about it. I am happy not to be on that strict budget like I was last week. But it sure was an eye-opener. I'm glad Tim had us do it."

"Me too. Although it's not quite as much fun now." She says with a smirk.

"By the way, I ran into a friend of mine who is an estate attorney and I asked her if someone in your situation who is about to get married should have a trust."

"Oh, that was so sweet of you. What did she say?"

"Well, of course, she said it would depend. Because I didn't give her much information and there's a lot more information she would need to be able to make a recommendation. But she says, in general, she does agree with Topaz that it would be important to protect what assets you have and creating a trust would be a great way to do it."

"Yes. I have been thinking a lot about that as well. Do you think Topaz would set that up for me?"

"Well, speak of the Devil," I said spying Topaz walking down the sidewalk coming the other direction.

"Tiiiiiiiiiiimmmmm!!" Irina yells across the sidewalk.

We all arrive at the bottom of the stairs the same time. Everyone gives each other kisses and hugs and tells everyone how great they look. And we slowly walk up the stairs together.

"Mel and I were just talking about you."

"I wondered why my ears were ringing. I hope only good things."

"Of course, who would have anything bad to say about you?"

Topaz laughed a very hearty laugh.

Irina excitedly asked "Will you set up a trust for me?"

"I can't set up a trust for you but I can definitely recommend a couple of estate attorneys I work with regularly that could set one up for you. What changed your mind?"

"Well, I did not like the thought of planning for my marriage to fail when you brought it up. But now that I have given it some thought it seems smart to protect myself in the event of who knows what. Isn't it true that if we're married and someone sues David's company that I could lose my own money?"

"That's possible. I couldn't really answer that because for one I'm not a legal professional but for two I don't know how his company is structured. But it's certainly a possibility. It's smart of you to consider the trust."

At this point we are all gathered in the hall near the elevator and other people are in the lobby.

"Why don't we all go to our apartments and change it to something more casual and we can go for a quick walk and discuss this further."

"That sounds like a great idea!" says Irina. She turns to me and asks "Will you come too?"

Surprised that she wanted me to come along I said yes. So we got into the elevator and press our respective floors. We agreed to meet downstairs in the lobby after we changed clothes.

Moments later I was downstairs in the lobby and Topaz was already there.

"How was your day, Darling?"

"It was good. I called HR like you suggested and as it turns out I wasn't maximizing the free money available to me. So I made that change."

"That's great. It's always good to take advantage of employee benefit programs and 401K matching is one of the most common ones that's offered."

"Thank you so much for suggesting that. I thought I was maximized but I guess not."

"You're welcome. I would advise checking once a year with your HR people to confirm your benefit status. Sometimes they make changes and while they do communicate this to the employees it may not always stand out or it may slip your mind. So it's a good thing to confirm every year."

"That makes sense. What's going on with you?"

Just then the elevator doors opened and Irina skipped out of the elevator. She was always so bubbly it was a joy to be around her.

"Is everyone ready?" Asked Topaz.

Irina and I both nodded and the three of us headed out the lobby. It was a gorgeous day and the promenade was even more crowded than normal with people zooming by on skates and scooters and bicycles and just generally enjoying the outdoors.

"Mel asked an attorney friend of hers if I should get a trust and she said yes." Irina tells Topaz.

"I said it depends!" I quickly interjected.

"Yes. Same thing." laughs Irina.

"I asked my friend if there was a down-and-dirty rule about when to get a trust and when it's not necessary. Her response was that if you have kids or a mortgage you should have one. But that's coming from her perspective I'm not sure if that's quite accurate."

"I agree" says Topaz, "Although that is a pretty good rule of thumb."

"But I don't have either of those" says Irina.

"Just because you don't have a mortgage doesn't mean you don't have a house to protect."

I looked at Topaz questioningly. Topaz looks at Irina. Irina nods back to Topaz as if some silent approval was being asked.

"Irina has a couple of properties. She was also left a considerable inheritance."

"Oh, I didn't know."

"Well, I wouldn't say considerable." says Irina humbly. It was a fair amount but I had numerous expenditures to make. But I do have some property that has been in the family for several generations."

"Well, then that makes a lot of sense for you to get a trust. That property would be a tragedy to lose that in a divorce were that to happen or even to lose it to a lawsuit. You never know what can happen. You could be driving along with a rental car and your insurance doesn't cover an accident and next thing you know there's a lien on your property."

Topaz chimes in. "If you put the house is in the trust they won't belong to you they will belong to the trust. And that will make it much more difficult for someone to get it in a lawsuit."

"What are some of the other reasons people get a trust?" Asks Irina.

"Well, a great thing about a trust is that you can now use the trust as your beneficiary. So let's say you get married and your husband is your beneficiary on your IRA. But then you get divorced and forget to change him as your beneficiary. Years pass and now you're remarried. Could you imagine forgetting about that old IRA and upon your passing your current husband finds that you left your money to your ex-husband?"

"You're getting a little head of things aren't you? I'm not even married once yet" Irina says.

"No. I see what she's saying. If you put the trust as a beneficiary on all of your investments then you only have one thing to update. So you change your trust and every single other investment changes as well because the trust is the most current piece of information."

"Right." says Topaz, "Sometimes people just use a trust to avoid expenses and time in probate and it can, in some cases, even lower taxes when leaving property to heirs."

"So it's just another level of protection against you and the bad guys?"

"That's an oversimplification but basically yes. I like it in your situation because you have property before the marriage that's been in your family for many years and you want it to stay in your family. A trust will help you do that."

"But if I didn't have the property or any money I wouldn't necessarily need to trust just because I was getting married, right?"

"Correct. If there was a one-size-fits-all plan for every single person then a computer could do my job. A lot of times with a financial advisor you're primarily using them for their expertise. Obviously all the information is out there on the internet but it's how it's interpreted and experience that shows you how to use it. Just like going to the doctor versus trying to diagnose yourself using WebMD. You're paying for the doctor's expertise and training."

WHAT'S NEXT?

Topaz, Irina and I continued walking along the promenade discussing trusts, investments and financial planning in general. It was really great to talk freely about these things without fear of judgement. I have never had "adult" conversations like this with my girlfriends. I began to wonder why it is that men brag about their investments all the time but women generally don't. At just that moment I was snapped out of my thoughts by something Topaz asked.

"What do you think, Mel?"

"About what?"

"Grabbing dinner or happy hour? I have my wallet if you didn't bring yours."

"I am going to see David in about an hour," interjects Irina as she glances at the time on her phone. "In fact, I should probably start heading back to the building so I have time to shower before I meet him."

"No, problem, Irina. Mel, are you in?"

"Sure, why not. Some place casual though." I said conscious of my workout attire.

"Of course, there's a cute place just over there." Topaz says while pointing in the opposite direction of our building.

"OK, you girls go and have fun, I'm heading back to the building." says Irina, clearly anxious to get home.

"Have fun with David." I say giving her an air kiss.

"Tell him we said 'Hi'," says Topaz saying goodbye to Irina.

"Will do." and with that Irina went towards the direction of the building.

Topaz and I walk towards the direction she pointed to the restaurant. We were there in no time. While it was lively, the restaurant wasn't overly crowded and we were seated right away.

It was a cute little sushi place I had never noticed before. The server put down our menus and asked for our drink orders. Before I could say anything, Topaz ordered a boat of sushi for us to split and a bottle of sake. She glanced at me as if asking for permission while server paused with her pen on paper awaiting my response.

"Sounds good to me." I said handing my menu back to the server.

"So what do you think?"

"About what? This restaurant?"

"Oh, this place is adorable. Just wait til you try their sushi. No, what do you think of the financial information we have been discussing?"

"I think it's great. I have never had these types of discussions before especially not with other women."

"Yes, that's a shame, isn't it? Women are always very supportive of other women but it's rare to have serious conversations about money with your female friends. Usually the only time money comes up is if we found some amazing deal at Bloomie's or whatever. We tell our friends about the deals and steals we find or the BOGOs that are coming up but never are bragging about the returns on our investments or how we are setting ourselves up for our future."

"I know. I mean basically since you got back to New York, you have done nothing but open my eyes to my spending and saving habits. I wish I had this conversation years ago!"

"Don't beat yourself up about time wasted. You're on the right path now."

"The other thing is that I really haven't taken retirement seriously. I mean it's so far off it isn't even something I am thinking about yet. A lot can happen in 20-30 years."

"I agree with you. Thinking about retirement planning when you're in your 20s and 30s seems foreign, especially if you're not married or your career is just getting started. Here's the thing to keep in mind though, you can finance many things in life but retirement isn't one of them."

"I never thought about it like that. . That's a good point. I am definitely making some changes to my spending and savings habits. I think all of us are, don't you?"

"Absolutely! I mean look at Francesca, she's making serious bank and was not saving any of it. Now that she has made a few tweaks in her lifestyle if she continues on the same path she could be semi retired by her 40s. She told me how upset she was that she has been blowing so much money just because she had it to spend. Now she's being a lot more responsible with her money and has already started putting some of it into investments."

"Really? That's great she's making changes. What did she do?"

"Well, first she moved to another apartment and the money her company is giving her for living expenses covers her living expenses, none comes out of her pocket. She decided to sell her car since she's living in Manhattan which I know was a hard decision for her coming from LA. And since she doesn't qualify for a Roth, I've put her in a cash value life insurance policy that she's overfunding."

"Wow. That's really great. I'm a little jealous!"

"Why? You're doing good too. You're paying attention to how much money you spend on a weekly basis. You're saving hundreds of dollars a year on your bagel addiction. You've made that call to HR and now will be getting hundreds of dollars a year of free money you were previously missing out on and you've hired a great financial advisor!"

"That's true. I also cut down my personal trainer so I'm saving thousands of dollars a year with him. I'm also bringing my lunch a couple days a week and I modified my cell phone plan. I just looked at all the areas I spend money in hopes to have more to save."

"That's fantastic! None of those changes sound particularly painful either. Being aware of your spending is great, but making changes is what it's all about. Like I said, just buying your bagel from a cheaper guy makes a big difference in the long run."

"I know and it sounds like Irina is really making changes too. I'm glad she is going to get a trust set up. I didn't know she had property to protect."

"Yes, she has changed her tune about money as well. As smart as she is I am a little surprised she was just going to leave her financial future up to her husband to provide. But now she's entering into the marriage with a clearer understanding of what she has and hopefully what he has as well so there won't be any surprises later."

"That is really awesome." I said.

"It is. I'm happy that I bought those ledgers for you two to use."

Remembering the week of the $300 budget I set for myself, I inwardly groaned. Tim laughed at my groan.

"I wasn't happy with the ledger."

"No, you weren't happy with the budget you set. The funny thing is that even if you had said a budget of $500, you still would have struggled. Most people will spend as much as they have. It's very difficult to show restraint if you don't have a reason to do so."

"Oh, you mean like how after I do some serious food shopping I eat everything in my apartment in like two days?" I said laughing.

"Unless you have a cute LBD to fit into for an event right around the corner." points out Topaz.

"True." I said considering the scenario. "It really is hard to be disciplined if you don't have a reason or goal set."

"Yes, but lucky for us, women are much better at saving than men. If we learn to invest as well as we save, we will rule the world!"

I think about this for a minute and nod in agreement. Mentally I make a note to come up with a dollar amount I can save each week or each paycheck so that it can go into investing for my future.

"So what's next?" I ask.

"What do you mean what's next? What's next for what?"

"Well what's next for me? I'm saving more money, I'm investing more money but what am I supposed to do next? What should Francesca do? Or Irina? How do we know what our next steps are going to be?"

"That all depends. The most important thing your financial advisor can do is to understand your objectives. Do you want to retire early? Do you want to save a bunch of money and go live off the land in one of those tiny houses? Do you want to retire to the South of France? Do you want to work forever because you love what you do? You can't answer the 'what's next' question without knowing what you want to do and what your goals are."

"That's fair enough. I suppose not everyone's idea of retirement is the same, is it?"

"Not at all. Gone are the days that you retire at 65, live off your pension and spend the rest of your life spoiling your grandkids. People now have many different ideas of retirement. Some may be semi-retired or have passive sources of income. Some go to warmer climates in the winter and spend that time fully retired and then when they return home they focus on their business again. With the Gig Economy, some may live partially off their investments and do short term work to supplement. I'm seeing a lot of doctors who want to retire in their 50s and together we're setting up ways to supplement their retirement income. That way, right now while they're working hard and don't have time to spend their money, they're letting their money work for them. Later, when they're ready to slow down, they'll be able to retire comfortably even though they're too young to touch their retirement accounts."

I thought about this as our server arrived with our sake and poured us each a cup.

"To Financial not being an F-Word anymore" Topaz says raising her sake cup in a toast.

"Here's to financial plans!" I toast. I think I really meant it. Having a plan in place has made things less stressful for me, I sleep better and I feel more secure. I'm definitely happier now that I have a handle on my finances.

We clink cups, drink our sake and Topaz pours another cup for us each.

"Think about what I said a couple weeks ago about the different quadrants of money," continues Topaz. "If you always have money in each category, you're doing great. But how much money you have in each quadrant will depend on where you are financially. Things like when you plan to retire and how risk-adverse you are and, of course, what the economy in general is doing all will dictate where you put your money."

"How so?" I ask.

"Well, take Francesca, she isn't going to retire for 20+ years and she likes high-risk/high-reward scenarios. Don't you think her quadrants are going to look very different than yours?"

"For sure. I would be willing to put money into a high-risk investment once my retirement is funded better. I seriously don't think she is thinking about retirement at all; she's just getting started in the work place."

"Yes, so when we sit down formally and talk about your financial situation I'm going to ask a lot of questions so I can provide the right suggestions for you."

"How often would we need to meet 'formally'?" I asked using air quotes.

"I recommend people review their financial plan once a year. But if something happens like you're going to get married or you inherited money or you're going to buy a house, you'd want to tell me about it because we may need to tweak your financial plan. If you have life events you contact me, if there are economic events, I contact you. Otherwise an annual review is adequate."

"What if the market crashes?"

"What if it does? We know it will, at some point, eventually. The goal is to be diversified enough that a huge market crash isn't going to affect you in a way that's going to derail you from your financial objectives. We are due for a correction in the not too distant future which is why planning for it will take the stress out of the equation. Too many people walk around with this feeling of impending doom but don't do anything to prepare for it."

About this time our sushi arrived and Topaz ordered another bottle of sake for us. The sushi boat looked amazing with many varieties of fish on display. I couldn't wait to sink my teeth into a piece of maguro that was staring at me.

"Thank you so much!" said Topaz to our server.

"Yes, thank you, it looks amazing."

"Enjoy it and I'll be right back with your sake." said the server.

"So I guess to answer my own question as to what's next, the answer is it depends."

Topaz nods in agreement with her mouth full of sashimi.

"Do I need life insurance? Should I get long term care? Do I roll over my own 401k into an annuity? Do I buy individual stocks or invest in mutual funds? Do I want to invest in a REIT? How much money do I need to have liquid? Should I buy gold? All of these questions can't be answered until I know what I want to do, what retirement means to me and how much risk am I willing to take. Right?"

"Yes, you've got it down. But first you have to have money to invest in and if you're not saving money currently then you need to start. Start conservatively though because you want it to be an amount you can accomplish comfortably every month. Like if you think you can save $500 a month for investing, just invest $300 for the first two months and hold the other $200 aside. You want to make sure it doesn't put you in a bind. It's terrible to have to pull money out of an investment in a hurry, even if there aren't any fees or penalties, you may take a loss. If, after two months, you still have that $200 lying around, then increase your budget to $500 a month. My guess is that once you see your investments growing that you're going to get excited and want to put more money into it. It's a great way to have your money working for you."

"That makes sense. Right now it is difficult to get excited about investing, especially for retirement. Money I can't touch isn't very interesting to me."

"True, but having money working for you is awesome. Have you ever read the book The Richest Man in Babylon?"

"No. Never heard of it."

"It's a quick read and worth picking up. Basically it just says how having your money work for you is the best way to create and preserve your wealth."

I picked up my phone and added the book to my Amazon cart before I forgot about it. Topaz was stabbing at something that looked like octopus. I picked up a piece of bbq'd unagi, at least I thought that they barbequed eel, it's cooked and delicious which was all I needed to really know.

"Thanks so much for teaching me all these things. I hope everyone has a good financial advisor like you to talk to freely. I never knew who to talk to or even what to ask before we started talking."

"You're welcome! I find a lot of people in my industry use technical jargon to talk to their clients and it doesn't help people that are new to money and aren't sure what to do in the first place."

"I know. I've learned a lot just being able to ask a question and not feeling stupid for asking."

"Good. Happy to help."

I cradled another piece of sushi in my chopsticks from the rapidly disappearing boat thinking about all the things I've learned in the past few weeks about money. Knowing my spending habits, knowing the cost of things, being smart about when and where I make purchases, talking to my HR people to confirm I'm taking advantage of the benefits available to me, learning about alternative investments, all the ways to use life insurance, tax deferred retirement accounts and protected money. I knew this was just the tip of the iceberg but I also know that now I could have conversations with my other female friends about money so that we could slowly change the way women think. Budgets and Financial Plans aren't bad words after all.

I wonder what's next...

ABOUT THE AUTHOR

Dianna Moses lived in NYC working on Wall Street for over a decade. She had the opportunity to live in other countries while working for some of Wall Street's top firms which gave her a lot of perspective. When she moved to Scottsdale, AZ and focused her attention on the financial advisory and planning side she realized there was a huge difference in talking to men about money versus having the same conversation with women. As a strong-minded, independent woman she wondered why so many women often still defer to their man for financial planning. Her goal is to change the world by changing the way women plan for their future.

Dianna has a thriving wealth strategies practice in Scottsdale, AZ and works with clients all over the country. She is also a Certified Divorce Financial Analyst working with high net worth divorces and the financial difficulties that brings. Her clients primarily consist of athletes, women new to money and specialty physicians. Guiding people through unfamiliar financial landscapes, helping them plan their future and making sure their hard earned money is protected in a simple and easy manner is her goal.

The characters from in Shopping, Stilettos and the F word are fictional and also appear in her book Glitter, Vodka & Orgasms: The Secret Path to Bliss. Their personalities are a culmination of Dianna's friends and clients and are not depicting any one person.

In addition to her passion for the financial world, she also races motorcycles, loves to fight in the ring, explore new restaurants and meet new people over cocktails. When she's not in the gym or on her motorcycle she will be sporting 5" stilettos of some variety as she has never met a high heel she didn't like. She lives with her Doberman Handsome Havoc in Scottsdale until it's too hot in the summers to function and then she goes to Texas to cool off to visit family and friends.

Her goal is to help all women achieve greatness by handling their money better, protecting themselves for unexpected events and educating women in the world of finance.

www.ingramcontent.com/pod-product-compliance
Lightning Source LLC
Chambersburg PA
CBHW070233190526
45169CB00001B/172